Putting the
University Online

Putting the University Online

Information, Technology
and Organizational Change

James Cornford
and Neil Pollock

The Society for Research into Higher Education
& Open University Press

Published by SRHE and
Open University Press
Celtic Court
22 Ballmoor
Buckingham
MK18 1XW

email: enquiries@openup.co.uk
world wide web: www.openup.co.uk

and
325 Chestnut Street
Philadelphia, PA 19106, USA

First Published 2003

A catalogue record of this book is available from the British Library

ISBN 0 335 21005 8 (pb)   0 335 21006 6 (hb)

Library of Congress Cataloging-in-Publication Data
    Cornford, James, 1963–
    Putting the university online : information, technology, and organisational
change / James Cornford and Neil Pollock.
        p.   cm.
    Includes bibliographical references and index.
    ISBN 0-335-21006-6 – ISBN 0-335-21005-8 (pbk.)
    1. Education, Higher–Computer network resources.   2. Education,
Higher–Effect of technological innovations on.   3. Virtual reality in
education.   4. Distance education. I. Pollock, Neil, 1967–II. Title.

LB1044.87 .C674 2003
378′.00285467–dc21   2002074811

Typeset by Graphicraft Limited, Hong Kong
Printed by St Edmundsbury Press, Bury St Edmunds, Suffolk

Contents

Acknowledgements

This book could not have been written without the support of the Economic and Social Research Council (ESRC), principally through two grants. The first, a study of virtual universities (as part of the ESRC's Virtual Society? Programme), was carried out with Kevin Robins, John Goddard, Frank Webster and David Charles. The second, a study of students as users of information systems (grant no. R000223276) was carried out with Kevin Robins. We would like to acknowledge the input of our collaborators on these projects, in particular John Goddard and Kevin Robins. We would also like to thank those staff at all the universities we studied, particularly CM at North Campus, who allowed us to undertake interviews and ethnographic research. Further thanks should go to Steve Woolgar, director of the Virtual Society? Programme and to Ian McLoughlin at Newcastle School of Management.

An early version of Chapter 3 was first presented at the ESRC 'Virtual Society? Get Real' conference in Berkhamsted, UK (April 2000), and a version of Chapter 4 was first presented to the Association of American Geographers 97th Annual Meeting, New York, USA (27 February to 3 March 2001).

For Chapters 5, 7 and 8 we would also like to acknowledge the help of those IT staff at Big_Civic who allowed us to undertake interviews and ethnographic research. Thanks also to John Goddard who provided us with several insights into 'university life', and to Martin Gilfillan, who was also present during some of the interviews reported here. An early version of Chapter 8 was presented at the Research Centre for the Social Sciences at the University of Edinburgh. Thanks to those, especially Robin Williams, who commented and provided feedback.

Chapter 6 was originally prepared for the joint Annenberg and iCS Conference on New Media and Higher Education, University of Southern California, USA (27–30 October 1999).

Neil Pollock would also like to thank Chris Stokes for his continual emails, telephone calls and helpful suggestions, and, most importantly, Luciana D'Adderio for her intellectual and personal input into the research projects on which this book was written.

James Cornford would like to thank Christine Raschka and, of course, Jake who is always keen to help.

1

The Online Imperative

The university in crisis: collapsing boundaries

The university, as an institution, is in crisis. The demand for higher education, from both governments and citizens, appears to be set for an unprecedented expansion. One might therefore think that universities, as the prime, if not the only, suppliers of that service, might be in robust health, confidently facing a rosy future. What is more, the much heralded arrival of a knowledge-based economy might be thought to play directly into the hands of institutions which are centrally concerned with, among other things, the creation, maintenance and diffusion of knowledge. Surely, the university's time has come. Yet the one clear message, perhaps the only clear message, that can be derived from a perusal of the contemporary literature on the university its role, goals and future is that the university is in crisis. The university is variously described as: a 'ruined institution' (Readings 1996), reduced to pursuit of a hollow and illusory 'excellence'; it is an 'attenuated' institution struggling to deal with an 'age of supercomplexity' (Barnett 2000); it is perhaps even a 'dinosaur' (Noam 1995) in a new networked environment which favours other, more recently evolved and more agile creatures. In all such accounts of the contemporary university and its future trajectories, one feature is common: that information and communication technologies, and above all the Internet, are a significant element of the current condition.

This apparent consensus about the significance of the digital technologies for the university masks a much wider set of arguments about *why* they are so important. The new technologies appear variously as the principal threat to the future of the university, as its potential saviour and, increasingly frequently, as both at the same time. If the university is to survive in a wired and networked world, then it too must 'get with the program' and move online. First, then, we briefly explore the principal threats which the online world is understood to present to the university.

The online threat

How are information and communication technologies being seen as threatening to the institution of the university? At the most general level, information and communications technologies, and actors, practices and processes which they support, appear to destabilize almost all of the established certainties around which the university has been formed. Here we will focus on these claims of new uncertainties in just two arenas: the realm of knowledge and the realm of geography.

Knowledge, its production through research, its refinement through scholarship and its diffusion through teaching and learning, is perhaps the notion above all others around which the self-image, if not always the reality, of universities circulates. Yet it is here, perhaps, that the online world is seen as most threatening. When knowledge is available to anyone with a computer and network connection (still a fairly restricted group of individuals at a world scale), so the argument goes, the university's position as *the* gatekeeper to the world of knowledge is undermined. New sites of knowledge have sprung up, nowhere more thickly than around the new technologies. Universities now have to compete with corporate laboratories and global consultancies in the knowledge claims that they put forward – competitors who can claim a greater performative value for their kind of knowledge. Further, the academy's claim to a unique disinterestedness in the development of knowledge is no longer so widely accepted. The university's structure of faculties and disciplines appears to get in the way of, rather than sustain, 'the new production of knowledge'. While universities might cling to their role in accreditation of learning, even here the market value of a Microsoft® or Cisco certificate can be greater than that of a university degree. As Barnett puts it:

> The problem with knowledge for the modern university is *not* that knowledge has come to an end. Rather, it is that there are now many knowledges vying for a place within the university. It is not that the clerks have lost their monopoly over the production of high status knowledge; . . . it is that they have lost their monopoly over the definitions as to what is to count as knowledge.
>
> (2000: 35)

In short, the modern university is confronted with a postmodern environment (Smith and Webster 1997).

The online world is also seen as threatening another important point of reference for the university – its practical and conceptual geography. Here the boundaries that are seen as being destabilized are those of the campus, the region and nation. Abeles is, again, a typical voice:

> with the rapidly increasing sophistication, and decreasing cost, of virtual courses, the hegemony provided by geography has disappeared. With increasing numbers of 'on-campus' students enrolling in their

institution's virtual courses on the Internet, the move towards courses offered by other institutions is only a 'mouse click' away. This is true whether the 'other' institution is located in Djibouti or is part of a multi-campus system such as in California or New York.

(1999: 10)

Globalization, to use the word of the moment, is seen as having undermined the intimate relationship which the university has developed, in the latter half of the twentieth century with the nation state. Here, too, there is a huge literature (e.g. Scott 1998). What, for us, is significant is the waning of the unique relationship between the university and the (nation) state. For Readings (1996), for example, the 'university of excellence' (in every- thing, equally, from particle physics to car parking) is constructed on the ruins of the 'university of culture'. And that culture was, of course, a national culture. Writing with the United States in mind, Readings argues that the state-funded expansion of the university after the Second World War was driven, in the sciences by the defence budget (the protection of national culture from threats from overseas), in the social sciences by the needs of the expanding welfare system (the extension of citizenship to all citizens), and in the humanities by the need to define a canon of national culture. With the collapse of the Soviet Union, the checking of the expansion of the welfare state and the demise of the canon, this three-legged stool has been kicked from under the university. In these conditions, the nation state, everywhere the major paymaster of the university, has taken a much less indulgent attitude towards the university.

Yet if information technologies, through the processes of globalization and postmodernization, are seen as part of the 'problem space' within which the university is struggling, they also figure in most maps of the 'solution space'.

The online imperative

If information technologies destabilize boundaries, then they can also be used to shore them up. If they threaten to pull the university apart, then they can also bind it together. In this respect the online or virtual university has emerged as a potent vision for the future of higher education, utilizing new information and communications technologies (ICTs) to radically restructure higher educational provision and to re-equip the university for its new environment. What is generally envisaged in this scenario is a 'univer- sity without walls'. Freed from the confines of the campus and its region, the university becomes a 'virtual' institution consisting of little more than global connections of potential students (recruitment), learners and teachers (students and staff), employers (the careers function) and alumni, in terms of teaching and learning, and researchers, research funders and research users, in terms of the institution's research mission, all held together by

ICT applications. The vision is one of flexible, ever changing organizations for knowledge creation and distribution. The university as an institution appears to dissolve.

This agenda has implications for the whole university. In terms of teaching and learning, it envisions the separation or unbundling of the development of course materials (packaging), the assembly of students (recruitment), the provision of learning and the assessment of competences. With this unbundling, the university ceases to be an end-to-end supplier of the higher education process and may undertake one or more of these roles, with other organizations undertaking complementary functions. The university, then, becomes far more externally oriented, an intermediary on the global stage, acting as collaborator, client, contractor and broker of higher education services. Of course, the extent of unbundling varies for different sub-markets, being greater in postgraduate, vocational and lifelong learning than in the undergraduate 'rite of passage' market.

In terms of research, the vision is one in which research teams cross disciplinary, institutional and national boundaries. In part this arises from the growth of big science with its huge research teams and massive resource requirements, but it also builds on disciplinary traditions in all subject areas. More significantly, research increasingly involves working much more closely with users in what has been called 'the new production of knowledge' (Gibbons *et al.* 1994).

The administration of the university, too, is transformed in the visions of the virtual or online university. At the heart is this change is the provision of comprehensive information systems to support teaching and research networks. More significantly there is a shift from an administrative culture to a professionally supported academic self-management.

This vision certainly has a widespread appeal to a range of stakeholders in higher education. As Gladieux and Swail put it:

> today's expanding, interactive computer networks possess a power, promise, and allure that institutions, governments, corporations, the nonprofit sector and students are responding to in unprecedented ways.
>
> (1999: 8)

What we want to do in this book is to explore a little more deeply some of the implications of this vision and what it might mean for the universities and those who work and study in them. We also want to suggest that the route towards the online university is not as simple as is often presented and that, when the weary travellers arrive at their destination, the 'actually existing' online university may not bear much resemblance to the vision.

What is driving the rapid diffusion of this vision? First and foremost, there is the shift from elite to mass higher education taking the form of increasingly large proportions of 18–20-years-olds going on from secondary education to higher education. This phenomenon, observed around the globe, has not been accompanied by a proportional increase in the funding of higher education. This has led to a declining resource per student and a concomitant search by higher educational institutions (HEIs) for efficiency gains. New information and communication systems hold out the promise of such gains. They not only enable the effort of teachers, researchers and administrators to be spread across ever larger bodies of students, thereby allowing lucrative niche markets (for example in relation to overseas students and mature students) to be reached cost effectively but also to drive internal efficiency through more streamlined workflows and administrative processes.

Further, the online university is seen as a strategy for coping with the increasingly diverse student body. As higher education has expanded it has moved beyond an exclusive focus on the single, middle-class 18–24-year-olds, engaged in the traditional 'rite of passage', to encompass other social groups engaged in 'lifelong learning' (Silver and Silver 1997). Few of the new groups entering higher education find higher education affordable or relocation to a traditional campus university for three or four years easy. Thus an increasingly heterogeneous student body requires new forms of marketing, support and monitoring. Here, too, the online university holds the hope of being able to provide new forms of higher education more suited to the needs of 'non traditional' students.

The shift from an elite to a mass higher education system has also meant that learners are increasingly actively recruited rather than passively selected. Here the online university is seen as a tool for expanding the recruitment options of the university, both geographically into new and lucrative overseas markets, and in terms of new social groups in the domestic market.

What is more, students are increasingly seen not just as clients of the university but also as a resource for the institution, for example in terms of regional engagement (e g student community action) and as alumni who may be persuaded to help to fund the institution and who can provide valuable contacts for research and recruitment, as well as openings for new graduates. Institutions are therefore adopting a more institutional approach to their students. The online university, from this point of view, proposes the tools required to organize and maximize this new resource.

Finally, students are increasingly seen as discerning clients with an increasingly wide experience of ICT from the world of private services and from the spread of these technologies in the home and workplace. The incorporation of ICT spend per head figures into many of the influential university rankings, for example, is seen as shaping the choices of potential students. Here, too, the provision of online materials is widely seen as helpful to the image and recruitment appeal of the institution.

The online university is also seen as a means of responding to a further set of pressures. Foremost among these are the external pressures, applied by national governments and funding agencies, for quality assurance and accountability for earmarked funding. Here the virtual university is seen as having the capability to readily provide statistics and support for the claims of universities in the face of demands for accountability. For example, the ill-fated UK MAC initiative, a tailored information system for universities, was substantially driven by the demands of government agencies for fuller statistical reporting of university activities (Goddard and Gayward 1994).

Further pressures concern the increasing demand for universities to show greater responsiveness to the needs of business and the wider community (Goddard *et al.* 1994). These pressures operate in each of the spheres of activity of the university, for example in terms of more rapid curriculum development to meet the emerging demands from employers or the demand for more policy-relevant research. More significantly, however, these demands also imply the bringing together of teaching, research and cultural activities as national and regional economic and social development strategies increasingly look to the university as a key player and demand a coherent institutional response. Here the promise of the online university is that, with the use of ICTs, the university can smoothly interact with the whole range of regional stakeholders. What is more, ICTs can enable the disparate activities of the university to be drawn together and the institution to 'speak as one' in its interaction with other agencies.

Finally, there is an increasing tension between the demands of teaching and the demands of research on the staff of the university. In this respect, the application of ICT is widely seen as offering the possibility for under-pinning a new division of labour within the university, shifting much of the routine work of academic staff onto the technology and administrative system and thereby freeing up time for higher prestige research work and high quality interaction with students.

We would be very wary of accepting any of these claims at face value. For example, there is very little evidence of major cost saving associated with the provision of ICT-based higher education (HEFCE 1999; Gladieux and Swail 1999; CVCP 2000). What is more, studies show that online distance education is dominated by those who already have some university educa-tion and is overwhelmingly concentrated on narrow, vocationally oriented courses rather than attracting new entrants to higher education. As Mason has put it: 'although the rhetoric of virtual education is that it will extend to the disadvantaged, the remote, the housebound and the unemployed, those who are signing up for virtual education are the advantaged, the upwardly mobile, the "over-employed" . . . and the well educated' (1999: 77). The use of ICTs with students and alumni is unproven, and whatever the image benefits of ICTs, studies tend to show that students' relationships to the technology are more complex than is often supposed by institutional man-agers (Crook and Barrowcliff 2000; Crook 2002).

To summarize, the virtual or online university promises to provide the capacity for universities to respond to and manage the range of pressures and tensions which characterize their current position. With the aid of ICTs, it is suggested, the university can simultaneously respond to new global markets, meet the requirements of increasingly onerous national regulation and audit, and satisfy the demand for new local engagement requirements – forces that might otherwise pull it apart. We are frankly sceptical about these claims. Along with John Seely Brown and Paul Duguid we suspect that 'the idea of the virtual university . . . both underestimates how universities as institutions work and overestimates what communications technologies do' (Brown and Duguid 1995; see also Newman and Johnson 1999). Nevertheless, these claims have underpinned an expanding programme of initiatives and projects within traditional universities as they have sought to explore the virtual university ideal.

The most celebrated (or perhaps feared) examples of progress towards the vision of the virtual or online university are new, 'for-profit' institutions, mainly in the United States. The University of Phoenix or Jones International University, for example, are often held up as exemplars.[1] The significance of these 'new' institutions, however, lies not in their direct impact – they actually provide a tiny, although growing, proportion of higher education in the United States and elsewhere – but rather, in their indirect impact on HEIs, operating through the perceived threat to established institutions both in terms of their markets for students and in terms of their demonstration effect. They have thus added a new impetus and urgency to the body of experimentation and innovation with the use of ICTs within existing institutions. For example, a recent survey funded by the Committee of Vice Chancellors and Principals (CVCP) found that 41 per cent of UK universities saw ICT as critical for future development, and a further 38 per cent had ICT 'high on the agenda' (CVCP 2000: 18). It is in this traditional higher education sector that we would argue that the most quantitatively significant moves towards the online university are to be found – what we might call brownfield, rather than greenfield, sites. And it is with these brownfield sites, established universities attempting to go 'online', that we deal in this book.

Putting the university online

Why have we written a book about putting the university online? There is a huge literature on the role of technologies in higher education. What could we possibly add to this body of knowledge? What are the lacunae in this corpus which we seek to fill? First, we need to characterize the existing literature addressing the relationship between universities and ICTs. This body of work can, we argue, be crudely divided into two strands of literature.

First there are those works which seek to make a general argument about the relationship between ICTs and the whole field of higher education, seeking the big picture. This debate is very much future-oriented (structured around questions about what the implications of the technology *will* be) and, as a result, not much concerned with the empirical material except as rhetorical ammunition or data from which trends can be extrapolated. Much of this work overlaps with the more general debate on 'the future of the university' or 'the future of higher education', both of which generally give a large degree of influence to the capacities of the new technologies.

Indeed, this strand of work often says little about any real university, one of the diverse range of concrete institutions bearing that title, but discusses a strongly ideal-typical notion of the university or more broadly higher education. It also has a much stronger focus on the teaching and learning aspects of the university than on its scholarly, research or community engagement roles. While this body of work contains much that is of interest, it is also lacking in a number of respects. First, much of this work is based on rational arguments from first principles, or more commonly from a given set of assumptions, and is lacking in detailed or systematic empirical support. Second, much of this work starts from fairly entrenched positions in which the normative dimension bulks large from the start. In these accounts, ICTs may figure on the side of the angels as technologies of freedom, or they may be the work of the devil, instruments of social control. Only occasionally they may figure as both. But they are almost always presented as unified and monolithic. We seldom get much sense of the variety of technologies associated with the online world or a picture of where these various technologies come from or how they are shaped in use.

The second strand of work which we would identify is made up of a number of much more focused and empirically grounded studies of particular applications of particular technologies in particular educational institutions. This work is typically structured around the question of whether there is a statistically 'significant difference' between the educational effects (however measured) arising from 'online', or, more generally, technologically mediated, education and more conventional means of teaching and learning. The scale and longevity of this debate can be measured by examining the bibliography at http://teleeducation.nb.ca/nosignificantdifference/ Related strands of more empirically informed research are concerned with 'scholarly communication' and an even smaller, but rapidly growing, body of work on the roles which ICTs play in the research process. Once again, however, what is important to note in this body of work is the highly uneven focus of attention. Once again, the particular technologies are often presented as a given: there is little description of the online course or programme, as opposed to its effects. Once again, the dominant concern is with the teaching and learning, and less so the scholarly functions of the university, saying almost nothing about research. This strand of work generally has even less to say about the role of ICTs in community or industrial engagement or, vitally for us, the management and administration of the university as a whole. Yet any university is about all of these tasks, and thus the process of putting the university online must take them in account too. Thus, where the 'big picture' literature tends to deal with the relationship between the new technologies and higher education, it avoids the actual institutional-level, work focused on individual courses or the evaluation of individual projects also has little to say about the university as an institution.

To sum up, in terms that might be familiar from science studies, the first debate is concerned with changing paradigms and the 'big picture', generating a range of bold conjectures, whereas the second is much more akin to 'normal science', concerned with the structured falsification of more tightly defined particular claims. From our perspective, both these two bodies of work have their strengths and weaknesses. However, we want to focus on what we see as the important set of questions which falls, as it were, between them. What we want to highlight here are three points, each of which can be tied to one of the words in the title of this book.

Putting *the university online*

First, then, our emphasis is on the process of *putting* the university on line. This process rarely figures, or rarely figures centrally, in either of the two bodies of work discussed above. They are both focused around contrasts, implicit or explicit, between two states, the offline and the online, the present and the future. They have little to say about the processes by which one state is converted into the other. Thus, their debates are predominantly about the impacts and outcomes of the technologies *after* they have been implemented and they pay little attention to the actual process of designing and implementing the technologies themselves. In a term which we define more fully in the next chapter, the actual technology is regarded as a 'black box'. The tendency, then, is to see impacts where the technologies have been adopted, where they have been made to work, which always leads one to tell a history from the point of view of the winners, from a position that appears secure and well-established. But looked at from the point of view of those putting the university online, the situation is often very different. Far from being a stable outcome, the online university is a fragile achievement, at least to start with, and those involved in the process are often painfully aware that it could so easily have been otherwise, projects could have stalled, failed or been abandoned. Indeed, in both the literatures sketched out above, the considerable work – of various types – required to make, say, a videoconference-based multisite seminar, an online assessment system, or an online payroll system actually work, is often obscured. This is not, then, a book about online universities, but one about putting the university online – it is a book about processes not outcomes.

Putting the university *online*

In the second term of our title, our emphasis is on the university, understood as an institution. The notion of 'the university' is a notoriously slippery one. We have already criticized the equating, common in the literature on virtuality, of the university with higher learning, or more minimally with instruction for accreditation. For while the issues of teaching and learning bulk large within any university, they do not exhaust its scope of activity. Rather, the university, in our sense, is a multitasking organization in which teaching, scholarship, research and 'community service' are all important goals and in which the administration (or, increasingly, management) required to balance, sustain and support those roles, is a critical component.

The traditional university is conventionally, if mythically, thought of as a band of scholars coming together to pursue and disseminate knowledge, governed by a more or less collegiate model of organization, based around a complex structure of committees and with a high degree of individual and departmental autonomy. In this sense, the university as an institution tends to lack a clear identity, primarily existing in the heads of people who constitute it and a myriad of locally negotiated practices and interactions. The central social role of the traditional university has been to provide a place-based 'rite of passage' for entry into middle-class professions through its undergraduate, vocational and extramural provision, together with the provision of ideas-driven 'academic' research. In institutional terms, the university has thus been described as an exemplar of a 'loosely coupled system' (Weick 1976) characterized by a lack of clearly articulated policy and weak control over the implementation of policy (McNay 1995). The traditional university as an institution, we might say, often appears to be only virtually present. The traditional university has, however, proven to be not only highly flexible and responsive, in particular to financial incentives from government, but also highly rigid and resistant to changes which threaten its autonomy.

This ambiguity is apparent in the extent to which, as one moves around a university, the institution of the university is always, to a greater or lesser extent, 'over there'. Thus for the academics in their departments, laboratories and research centres, 'the university' generally refers to the senior management and, particularly, central administration. By the same token, for the senior management and the administrators, 'the university' which they are seeking to govern, manage and administer is very clearly 'out there' in the departments, laboratories and research centres. Meanwhile, for the students, 'the university' is seen as comprising both these groups, but once again somewhat distanced and apart. 'The university', even for those who work or study within one, is always 'them' and never 'us'. In many ways, this distancing is understandable. For the academic, both status and job security are dependent less on their current university and more on the 'invisible college' of academics in the same or cognate disciplines at other institutions. For the institutional manager or administrator, progress depends on interaction with a body which it is impossible to fully understand (for who can understand the physicist, the economist and the literary theorist equally well). And for the students, the duration of their sojourn in the university is typically still a fairly short-lived prelude to something greater.

Our own solution to the problem of defining the university is therefore not to attempt a general definition acceptable to all, but rather to accept the complex and multiple meanings of the term. For us, then, the institution of the university is a function of the everyday practices through which these loosely defined bodies are instituted, accepting that ambiguity and ambivalence must be part of an adequate definition rather than being the enemies of definitional clarity. Our view is a multi-perspectival view. Our focus is on the network of everyday action which, in spite of the different conceptions of the university, sustains the concrete institutions that we have studied. It is this perspective that leads us to draw on the notion of actor networks introduced in the next chapter and developed throughout this book.

Putting the university online

How do we understand the third part of our title? What does it mean to put an institution online? Here we confront the question of technology, drawing on wider debates about the role of technology and its relations to the social realm.

One tradition, still dominant in policy research, has been concerned with the impact of technology, above all ICTs, on social and economic life. This tradition has an economic bias and a predominantly extensive and quantitative empirical approach. However, in spite of the great claims that have been, and are still, made for the transformative capacities of new ICTs, some twenty years of research unambiguously suggests that 'ICTs rarely cause social transformations' (Kling *et al.* 2000: 65; cf. Webster 1995). Even in terms of an issue such as the economic impact of the diffusion of computers and the Internet on US productivity, where some of the claims for transformation have been loudest and much data is available, this is hotly contested (Gordon 2000; OECD 2000). (Indeed, the most interesting outcome of this debate has been a profound rethinking of the meaning of productivity.) More theoretically, the crude technological determinism and the notion of technology as an exogenous variable in social change, which characterized earlier work in this tradition, have become more and more untenable. In the face of these empirical and theoretical challenges, this tradition has increasingly focused on the context of diffusion, on the organizational and other social changes that are seen as necessary to release the potential of ICTs, leading to a concern with the development of complex socio-technical systems, and moving away from crude impact metaphors to an ever more subtle and baroque modelling of the relationship between technologies and society.

The alternative major tradition, and now perhaps the dominant tradition among academic social scientists, has focused on the ways in which social and economic processes and forces shape the form and content of technologies and services – the socio-economic shaping of technology or, more emphatically, the social construction of technology. This body of work, with its predominantly qualitative and fine-grained empirical approach, tells us a great deal about why particular technologies and services are the way they are, how they have been developed and deployed, and the crucial role of meanings and understandings in that process. By stressing the way in which

ICTs are shaped by powerful socio-economic forces, this tradition has helped to explain the lack of social and economic transformations noted by Kling and others. It is, however, often a highly focused and retrospective exercise which provides only hints and clues about the longer-run implications of technologies for the wider society and economy and is often of limited use in helping individuals and groups to make better decisions about ICTs (McLaughlin *et al.* 1999; McLoughlin 1999; MacKenzie and Wajcman 1999).

Both traditions, then, while having something to offer, appear increasingly exhausted. However, if we regard them dialectically as thesis and antithesis, then we might begin to construct some new synthesis, which can build on, but also take us beyond them both. From the first tradition, then, we want to take seriously the concern with the larger-scale, long-run transforming potential of socio-technical systems (and the limits thereof), while from the second we take the focus on meanings and understandings as the key to grasping that potential.

ICTs, like other goods and services, come into a particular community with powerful suggested meanings, or 'scripts' attached, constructed by their developers and marketers. Yet study after study has found that these supposedly dominant meanings fail, to a greater or lesser extent, to be translated into practice. Rather, they are contested, resisted, deflected or complemented by other meanings developed by their intended audience and others (Mackay *et al.* 2000). These meanings are, of course, deeply context dependent, building on and bound to established frames of reference and forms of practice. Thus the meanings of ICT emerge and are learned in the context of a specific situation and the network of individuals and institutions which comprise it. ICTs may, of course, have different meanings for different groups and the meaning of ICT may be contested within and between groups. It is, however, these meanings which most powerfully shape the ways in which particular institutions attempt to assimilate (adopt, adapt and use, or reject) particular ICTs.

For us, then, the process of putting the university online implies much more than a simple technical exercise in which some materials or processes are simply transferred from the offline world to some ready-made online realm. This, as we hope to show, is a complex process in which the meanings of, and boundaries between, online and offline are not pre-given but rather are actively constructed.

Structure of this book

The rest of this book is broadly structured to take a journey from the sub-institutional level, focusing first on the ways in which online technologies are inserted into relationships *within* the university, through a focus at the level of the institution itself – technologies and relations *across* the university – and culminating in a focus on the technological mediation of relationships *between* universities. As a preparation for this journey, Chapter 2 introduces our theoretical and methodological stance, drawing on work in science and technology studies, to elaborate our particular understanding of what it might mean to put the university online, introducing the particular institutions which we have studied and reflecting a little on the problems of seeking to do research in such institutions. The six substantive chapters which follow are intended to work in pairs.

- Chapter 3 is concerned with the kinds and volumes of work involved in constructing online courses, while Chapter 4 develops some of the arguments of Chapter 3 by focusing on the relationship between the physical campus environment and the new online technologies.
- Chapter 5 shifts the central focus to the higher education institution as a whole, questioning the dominant 'informational' understanding of the university, while Chapter 6 develops the arguments of Chapter 5 by focusing on the question of standardization associated with the informational view of higher education.
- Chapters 7 and 8 move the focus once again to the *inter*-university scale and the relationship between universities and other organizations. Chapter 7 explores the ways in which the university's engagement with ICTs raises the issue of the uniqueness of the university as an organization, distinct from other organizations. Chapter 8 explores both the ways in which putting the university online is deployed in strategies to mark a particular university as distinctive, and also the ways in which it creates forces to homogenize universities.

Chapter 9 reflects on and concludes the book.

Chapters 3 to 8 have been written to function as standalone essays and may be read in isolation by those readers who so prefer. We have, however, attempted to keep the repetition which this approach requires to a minimum in order to avoid irritating those who prefer to read a book from beginning to end. We hope that, given the gradual development of the arguments through the various chapters, this is the preferred mode of reading.

Conclusions

- Information and communications technologies (ICTs) are seen not only as threatening the university as an institution, deepening its sense of crisis, but also as holding out the promise of a solution to, or at least a way of living with, that crisis.
- The virtual or online university has emerged as a potent vision of one way of addressing the increasing demands placed on the university.
- While there has been much speculative writing about the impact of ICTs on the university, and a parallel literature of detailed studies or evaluations of particular online activities, these literatures have three significant lacunae:

- First, they are mainly concerned with online universities, eliding the prior processes of *putting* the university online.
- Second, they have a strong bias to address either higher education or specific aspects of teaching and learning, scholarship and, less often, research. They thus omit the question of the institutional-level analysis of the putting of *the university* as an institution online.
- Finally, much of the work has a strong (implicit) technological determinism and a narrowly technological understanding of the scope of the problem of putting the university *online*.

Note

1. Neither of these institutions provides the full range of courses typical of traditional universities, nor do they undertake research.

2

Researching Changing Universities

Introduction

How are we to study the process of putting universities online? How can we get a purchase on the changes that are occurring within institutions, given the scale and complexity of the higher education sector and the various technological projects under way? In order to make visible what are manifold and complex processes of change and innovation – work that includes the development and shaping not simply of artefacts but also of meanings, boundaries, processes, actors and practices – we have chosen to adopt an intensive ethnographic approach, and to illuminate this through drawing on work from the sociology of science and technology, particularly but not exclusively the actor network tradition. In this chapter, while not wishing to enter into a lengthy discussion about the merits or otherwise of ethnographic research, we intend to say something about its principal features as we understand them. We then introduce our theoretical approach before outlining some of the more practical aspects of the research.

Ethnography

An ethnographic study suggests a long-term involvement in a particular field site, during which time various methods are deployed to understand and participate in the relationships and activities ongoing in that setting. The aim of this activity is to say something about the various, often tacit, ways in which the subjects of the ethnography organize their lives. Hammersley and Atkinson, for instance, outline a common understanding of ethnography:

> In its most characteristic form it involves the ethnographer participating, overtly or covertly in people's daily lives for an extended period of time, watching what happens, listening to what is said, asking questions

– in fact, collecting whatever data are available to throw light on the issues that are the focus of the research.

(1995: 1)

Although ethnography casts its net far and wide in terms of where it looks for insights, it also insists on the deployment of caution or 'analytical scepticism' about what it finds. Rather than accept everything at face value, Hammersley and Atkinson argue, the ethnographer should deploy a 'self-conscious awareness' of what is learned, 'how it has been learned', and the 'social transactions that inform the production of such knowledge' (1995: 101). Drawing on John Law's (1994) ethnography of a laboratory, we might say that ethnography is interested not in finding one 'true account' (as if this were at all possible or desirable) but in the different 'stories' that people tell about their organization, its history as well as the changes occurring within it. As Law writes: 'people in the Laboratory formulate and they tell stories of themselves and one another – layer upon layer of stories' (1994: 19).

Allied to this is a claim for the suspension of common sense or theoretical knowledge about a setting. This, perhaps, is one of the most appealing features of ethnography in that it promises access to the issues, concepts and categories that are deemed relevant by those in the field and not imposed *a priori* by the researcher. This principle has been deployed to interesting effect by sociologists of science and, more recently, actor network theorists who have argued for a suspension of belief about defining truth and falsity in scientific disputes or the social and technical dimensions of a technology if the nature of these phenomena are still being negotiated by those under study (Callon 1986b). Suspension of belief about what is good or bad science or where the divide between society and technology begins and ends turns what is typically a resource to be drawn upon into a topic that is to be studied (Grint and Woolgar 1997). In an intriguing study, Rachel (Rachel and Woolgar 1995) has attempted to observe the 'technical work' of software developers. To her surprise she is continually told, 'No, I don't do really technical work', and is directed to someone else in the organization. On arrival at the next site, where, she was assured by her original contact she would be able to observe 'technical work' in progress, she receives the same response and is directed on once again. This leads her to conclude that, in this organization at least, the real technical work is *always* done elsewhere. Refusing to impose a conventional understanding of what technology or 'the technical' might be allows Rachel and Woolgar insights into the ways in which these people negotiate and allocate responsibilities for their work that otherwise would not be possible.

All of this is not to say, however, that we entered the field site without certain assumptions or 'sensitizing concepts'. Rather than adopt the prevailing notion of technology evident in our field site, for instance, as Rachel and Woolgar do in their ethnomethodology-influenced study, we worked with a broader notion influenced by recent work within the sociology of science and technology and the actor network approach. We did this in order to avoid falling into line with ontological definitions prevailing in our field site. For example, the aim of this book is to show how ICTs shape universities and how ICTs are themselves reshaped in that process. As we see it, neither the status of the university nor the technologies are fixed: as ICT projects are introduced into the university system their consequences are the outcome of a complex process of negotiation, involving interactions within a heterogeneous network of actors, artefacts and systems. In this process both the university and the technology will change. Below we set out a number of commonplaces for studying technology. We do this both as a way to introduce the reader to (or remind the reader of) some of the literature within the sociology of science and technology, and, as is common in ethnographic studies, as a means to consider and articulate some of the assumptions that we have carried into our field site.

The sociology of science and technology

As we have hinted above, it is increasingly the case that technology is viewed not as separate from, but rather made up of, social relations (including culture, politics, economics etc.). Historians and sociologists of technology have argued that there is little analytical purchase to be gained from continuing to talk about the 'social' and 'technical' as if they were independent entities. Rather, as they and many others see it, the social and technical are inextricably entwined. Technologies and all the social elements that constitute them are often described as 'seamless webs' (Hughes 1986), 'networks of humans and non-humans' (Latour 1987), or 'socio-technical ensembles' (Bijker and Law 1992).

Once we refuse to separate the social from the technical then what follows is an alternative way of conceptualizing the innovation process. Law (1987), among others, has painted a picture of innovation where the principal actors not only engage in those practices typically thought to belong to 'science' or 'technology' but also operate as multifaceted entrepreneurs or 'heterogeneous engineers' who bring to bear whatever approach (political, economic, social) or resource (legislative, financial, rhetorical) is deemed appropriate to get their work done. Moreover, it has been suggested that the most successful innovators are those who concern themselves not simply with physical objects but who simultaneously construct the 'social world' or 'context' into which their objects will be inserted. In this respect, Latour (1988a) has eloquently described how the scientific work of Louis Pasteur and his Institut Pasteur was, on the one hand, concerned with the production of a serum against diphtheria and, on the other, with the recruitment of allies (hospitals, physicians, horses and the diphtheria bacteria itself) to support and underwrite the serum. The construction of one of these sides is, as Latour has argued, just as important as the construction of the other. This is a theme we discuss throughout the book, particularly in Chapter 3.

There has been much valuable theoretical and empirical yield from this early work, leading to the development of a conception of technology which is sometimes called co-production or co-construction.[1] One area where this approach has found much applicability is among those interested in the relationship between the 'producers' and 'users' of technology. The notion of co-production has revived interest in what had become a rather stale debate concerning the question whether technology determines the shape of society (i.e. technological determinism) or society determines the shape of technologies (i.e. social determinism).[2] Akrich's (1992) article on an electricity generator used by villagers in French Polynesia is among those that most clearly articulate an attempt to treat symmetrically technology and society. We review it here in some detail as it underpins the perspective adopted in Chapter 5, where we discuss attempts to redefine a university, and Chapter 8, where we discuss how a new view of the student is rolled out along side a new student management system.

Akrich's argument is that the design of a technology simultaneously requires the 'design of the user', that is, a user's skill, their abilities and what the technology should do in relation to the user are 'scripted' into an artefact and this influences its final shape. This is not to say that it is a simple matter of outlining a better description of those who are to use the technology, however. Rather, according to Akrich, the 'user' does not pre-exist the technology but is actively constructed alongside the object. In other words, the introduction of the technology may well be intended to contribute to the construction of a new kind of user, one with different characteristics, roles and responsibilities. Akrich explains this notion further:

> A large part of the work on innovators is that of 'inscribing' [a] vision of (or prediction about) the world in the technical content of the new object . . . [D]esigners thus define actors with specific tastes, competencies, motives, aspirations, political prejudices, and the rest, and they assume that morality, technology, science, and economy will evolve in particular ways.
>
> (1992: 208)

While the preceding argument has been somewhat abstract, Akrich does provide an extended discussion. The generator had a major limitation: when the photoelectric cells powering it were running low (as often happened), there was a likelihood of serious damage if electricity was continually drawn. Engineers, therefore, installed an automatic 'control device' which would cut power to the village when the cells were too low. Akrich describes how the assumption by the engineers was that the villagers could not be trusted to monitor and control use of the battery. The control device was therefore a way both of safeguarding the generator of disciplining villagers' use of it. Of course, this does not mean that a technology cannot be changed or that the villagers had to subscribe to the script. Importantly, out of frustration from constant power cuts the villagers eventually worked around the control device by employing a local electrician to install a temporary fuse. All of this points to the way in which the introduction of a technology 'specifies' the shape of a user's environment, but it is, as Akrich argues, a multilateral process where users are able to renegotiate the nature of that specification through their own user modifications (see Chapter 6). To return to our original co-production theme, what we have been describing is the simultaneous shaping of a technology and building of society (cf. Bijker and Law 1992).

Actor network theorists have similarly argued for an approach that brings together and, importantly, treats in a symmetrical way the social and the technical. They have developed the notion of an 'actor network', which attempts to trace out the relationships humans have not only with each other but also with non-human actors and entities. Drawing on semiotics they designate all actors as 'actants' in order to emphasize the point that non-humans (animals and things) are also included in the analysis. Moreover, actor network theorists have developed a variety of terms to conceptualize how such actor networks get built. One central idea is that humans and non-humans are enrolled into a network through a process of negotiation or 'translation', which is made up of several key moves. First, there is *interressement*, which is a form of 'problematization' or the way one actor raises an issue about the identity or goals of another. Next, there is *enrolment*. This is the process whereby an actor or organization has his or her identity or goals changed or diverted. Finally, once an actor accepts the identity or goals of another then actor network theorists commonly speak of *network alignment* or *stabilization*. This is the phase in which all participants are 'saying the same thing' on the topic with which they are mutually involved (Callon 1991). Once a network achieves a stable and solid identity, all its constituent nodes tend to fade from view as the network becomes connected to other actor networks.

Another, perhaps clearer, way of putting this is to think of a technology as becoming 'black-boxed'. That is, all previous discussions, questions, assumptions and, maybe, controversy are closed down and are no longer visible as the technology moves from a private to a public domain. Woolgar, for instance, discusses the (literal) black-boxing of a new personal computer. At the manufacturer, he writes, it was common to find computers being used without their covers. Once a machine was to be introduced to users, however, as in the case of a usability trial, engineers would insist that the computer was packaged inside the case. The function of the case, he argues, was to ensure that the users accessed the computer in the 'appropriate manner':

> The video record of the usability trial shows putative users working out how to relate to . . . a technology which had already been black-boxed. Or, in this instance, beige-boxed. The task for the subjects of the usability trials was to work out how to access the interior of the beige box, in order to extract what they needed from the machine/company. The machine's task was to make sure these putative users accessed the

company in the prescribed fashion: by way of preferred (hardware) connections or through a predetermined sequence of keyboard operations.
(Grint and Woolgar 1997: 82)

There is a large and fruitful debate in the sociology of science and technology investigating the opening and closing of black boxes. Relevant to this
study, McLaughlin *et al.* (1999) suggest that software is one example of a
technology that, upon entering an organization, is reopened as questions
arise about its origins as well as its usability and suitability, before it is
reconstructed and black-boxed once again. This notion of opening and
closing a black box has relevance for this book, especially Chapter 7 where
we consider the introduction of an enterprise resource planning (ERP)
system. As in the study conducted by McLaughlin and her colleagues, questions are raised about the suitability of the ERP system and its applicability
in the context of a university.

The four field sites

The material presented here is based on research work carried out over
a four-year period. The first two years were carried out in the context of
a wider research programme, sponsored by the Economic and Social
Research Council (ESRC) and entitled 'Virtual Society?', which began in
1998. In line with our approach, we have concentrated our research on
particular higher education *institutions*, in order to pursue the nature of
their response to change. We chose to observe projects in four very different institutions, one of which was our own and all of which were in the
north east of England. At the conclusion of the Virtual Society? research
programme we were successful in winning further funding from the ESRC
and were able to continue our research, albeit this time choosing to continue to study only one of the institutions from the earlier study. However,
because the focus of that study was a global alliance with a large software
house and a number of universities abroad, we were able to extend the
reach of our research into the international arena.

Our choice of institutions was governed by the following criteria. First,
the universities in the region constitute a good cross-section of UK higher
education institutions: *Big_Civic* is a large red brick university with a full-
time student population of 12,000; *North_Campus* is a 'new' university with
15,000 full-time students; *City_Campus* is also a 'new' university with a full-
time student population of 15,000; and, finally, the *Open University*[3] is perhaps
the world's leading provider of university-level distance education with a
predominantly part-time student population of over 100,000. Second, each
of these sites is actively engaged in promoting the development of ICTs,
and, in many cases, is seen to be at the forefront of such innovation in
higher education. These universities are in the periphery of England and
ICTs provide new opportunities, such as access to information resources

concentrated in the Oxford–Cambridge–London triangle. Related to this, we wished to explore tendencies towards decentralization and disembedding, while also paying attention to the significance of the local culture – the university in the community (i.e. to balance a concern with virtual possibilities with a recognition of the commitment to place). Finally, our 'insider' status within the region gives us good access to developments within these four universities.

To get the research under way we began to identify technology projects within our field sites that might be of interest. In order to do this, and as a condition of our research funding, we brought together an advisory group – a number of senior academics, university managers and ICT practitioners – to find out their views on our research plan, to suggest possible sites and, if possible, help facilitate access. There were numerous suggestions, and we looked briefly at all of them before deciding on our final sites. In choosing projects for analysis, we were attentive to what we consider to be the primary aspects of change: the governance of universities; changing practices in teaching and research; and questions of space and place. The following appeared to meet some, if not all, of these requirements:

- At Big_Civic there was the development and deployment of a new management and administrative information system (the Enterprise project) based upon a SAP R/3 computer system; and related to this we followed the development of Campus Management, a software module currently being developed by SAP and implemented in a number of universities around the world.
- At North_Campus we focused on the activities of the Learning Development Services and Information Services (library). Three of the projects investigated were: a virtual seminar conducted with three other European universities; the development of an online degree module called Cyber Culture; and the conversion of a module taken annually by over 300 first-year students into an online self-study module.
- At City_Campus we have followed the development of a programme entitled 'Excellence in the Use of Communication and Information Technologies'.
- At The Open University we looked at the introduction of ICTs, and how they were changing relations between tutors and students.

In addition to the project noted above, both authors were previously involved in a number of other studies. Pollock, as part of his doctoral work, conducted research on the University Funding Council's Management and Administrative Computing (MAC) initiative, where he conducted a six-month ethnographic study at one site where MAC was being implemented. Cornford has conducted research under the Joint Information Systems Committee (JISC) Hybrid Libraries programme, involving both librarians and departmental research and teaching staff, building subject- or group-specific web-based interfaces to paper and electronic information sources. Both these studies have also influenced the shaping of the present work.

Through the eyes of designers

This section describes how we decided what and whom to look at. Again, we drew lessons from the sociology of science and technology and the actor network tradition. In terms of what should be studied, Latour (1987) has famously advocated that technologies should be studied not as finished artefacts (i.e. black boxes) but 'in the making', arguing that, by studying them in this way, the 'messiness' is still there for all to see. By messiness he means not only those issues identified by the researcher but also those that arise during the building and implementation of ICT projects. We studied, therefore, projects as they were actually being planned, built and used. For this, we made use of direct and participant observation where we attended project meetings, away-days, committee meetings, user-feedback and brain-storming sessions, technical briefings, presentations and travelled overseas to observe interaction between a major global software developer and an inter-national set of universities which were acting as pilot sites for the techno-logy under development. We also used more conventional semi-structured interviews, which we recorded and had transcribed.

In terms of 'who' is to be studied, Latour suggests 'following the actors', meaning those central to rolling out these technologies. Again these are not people identified by the researchers but are those deemed relevant by those actually building the technologies. Here we spoke to senior university managers, external consultants, project managers, practitioners, academics, administrators and support staff. While these principles have found wide-spread acceptance among the sociology of science and technology commun-ity they have also been subject to some criticism. Bowker and Star (1999) argue that while following the actors allows us to share in their insights it also means we share their 'blindness'. The actors being followed do not themselves see all the disorder their technologies bring: they construct the world in which this disorder occurs. McLaughlin and her colleagues (1999) echo this point when discussing the literature on the users and producers of technology, arguing that following only technology-builders means that users will only ever be seen from a limited point of view or through the 'eyes of the designer'. It is because we wanted to situate the implementation of these ICT projects in the multiple networks of the university that, as well as following those actively involved in the technical work, we also followed users, future users and those who might only be indirectly affected by the technologies.

Here we often met these people in groups, as it was felt that if we were to approach each person individually then it might be difficult to get them to talk about a system or technology for which they as yet had little detail. Thus, it was (correctly, as it turned out) imagined that as part of a larger group, the future users might be more open to discussion. For instance, we were able to conduct a series of focus groups with secretarial and non-academic support staff that had recently undergone, or were about to undergo, training on the enterprise-wide computer system. Here they swapped information on what they believed the system might mean for working practices in their particular departments. We also talked to trade unions who similarly had concerns about changing work practices, and to groups of academics who were participating in a new virtual seminar. Finally, to supplement the information gained we also collected and read from many documentary sources.

Research and reflexivity

There is a final set of actors that we have as yet not identified: namely, the authors of this book. One outcome of our 'close in' approach, and also of our decision to study our own institution, was the way in which we (as researchers) began to be enrolled into the various projects that we were studying. This ranged from a peripheral involvement (Pollock was invited to be the external auditor on one of the online modules that he had been following; Cornford was asked to lead a session at a workshop organized by a major software supplier's universities research user group), to a central engagement (where one of our colleagues and research collaborators became the project director of the technology that we were studying). It is worth spending some time describing the latter example, for it has been extremely valuable in terms of highlighting both the intellectual and the practical issues a researcher might face when conducting research on home ground, as it were, and the increasingly blurred boundary between the 'researching' and 'doing' of ICT projects.

Shortly after beginning our study, one of the team was appointed to the position of pro-vice-chancellor, with responsibility for the implementation of a management information computer system across the university, the same system that we had decided to study. This had two highly related consequences. First, our colleague, in his new position of pro-vice-chancellor was simultaneously having to act in two seemingly distinct worlds – as manager and as researcher; and, second, because of this, it was brought to our attention that the boundary between our research world and the world of those whom we were studying was incredibly flimsy, if it was there at all (cf. Woolgar 1988). One consequence of this was that the pro-vice-chancellor was able to deploy insights learned from our research to (what we hope was) good effect in the practical work of rolling the system out, while providing us with insights and access which we would not have otherwise had.

At a more general level, the ways in which we became actors in the dramas which we were trying to study has led to a heightened awareness of our own status as social scientists and encouraged us to think about our research not simply as an attempt to throw light on processes of change within universities but in terms of whether the 'work' that we were doing helped or hindered the building of the online university. For instance, at one advisory group meeting arranged as part of our Virtual Society? project, we realized as the participants were chatting among themselves at the end, that we had brought together various actors who were now discussing the possibility of future collaborations. Similarly, having visited one particular university department several times, we were told by a developer that his boss had recently decided to devote more resources to technology initiatives. When we asked why, he replied that it was our presence that had finally convinced her. Seemingly, the issue of the online university as she saw it had suddenly become a 'hot topic', and one in which their university should be investing.

Conclusion

In this chapter we have sketched out the basic framework of our approach to studying the process of putting the university online. It is, of course, not the only approach, and we leave it to the reader to decide if it is at least a fruitful and insightful approach. However, one implication of our decision to adopt an ethnographic approach is the acceptance that theories, whether ours or other people's, are always rooted in particular circumstances and histories. As a result, we return in the following chapters to many of the themes introduced here. We do so in a way that is not, we hope, too repetitive. Rather, we seek to ground the themes more firmly in the situations that we have studied.

Notes

1. For one of the best examples of co-production see Berg's (1997) article on healthcare technologies and how they are implicated in the production of nursing work.
2. For the classic example of the former see Daniel Bell's (1976) *The Coming of Post-Industrial Society*. For the latter see Donald MacKenzie and Judy Wajcman's (1999) *The Social Shaping of Technology*.
3. While we have masked the identity of our first three universities, we have not attempted to hide the identity of The Open University (OU). This is because its unique status would enable the OU to be easily identified no matter which pseudonym we chose. Also, our research in the OU was fairly limited, given our interest in more traditional university sites. We therefore concluded that anything we wrote was unlikely to be embarrassing to the university.

3

Working through the Work
of Making Work Mobile

The hype of our times is that we don't need to think about the work anymore.
(Bowker and Star 1996)

Introduction

What does the recent application of information and communications technologies (ICTs) in higher education, and particularly the emergence of digital, online or virtual universities hold for the future shape of established, campus-based universities? The transformative and increasingly popular view is that because of the possibility of new and different ways of producing, distributing and consuming higher education, these new 'placeless' institutions have the potential to reshape traditional university geographies, as well as their methods, relationships, and perhaps even 'ethos'. With widespread access to the Internet, it is argued, scholars and students no longer need to travel in order to join together for learning and study. All the resources of the university – libraries, lectures, seminars, tutorials – can be moved online and accessed from any networked computer terminal. Told in such a manner, it is perhaps easy to be seduced by suggestions that we are nearing 'the end of campus-based education' (Noam 1995: 247–9), or that the key university function – the creation, preservation and transmission of knowledge – is to be rapidly usurped by telecommunications networks (broadcasting, cable, Internet, World Wide Web, email, etc.) (Abeles 1998).

For all that has been written about them, however, recent research suggests that virtual institutions represent only a tiny fraction of higher education provision. Their significance therefore lies not so much in their real-world number or market share, but in the pressure they bring to bear on the mainstream higher education sector to adopt methods, strategies, technologies and, perhaps, the more commercial ethos of these virtual and typically corporate providers.[1] Having caught the imagination of policy makers, institutional managers and academic leaders (see, for example, Newby 1999), it would seem that universities everywhere are embarking upon ambitious plans to translate established modes of provision into ones that can be delivered via technology and at a distance.[2] Indeed, such is the enthusiasm and activity under way that some suggest a 'blurring of the boundaries between distance education and on-campus teaching' (Johnston 1999: 39). Given that the bulk of the work of building ICTs into higher education is taking place in existing and established institutions, then, the question that begs an answer is: how are traditional universities attempting to come to terms with these new technologies?

Here, much of the recent writing on universities is limited, assuming either a 'pro' or an 'anti' stance, and tending to emphasize only the differences that exist between online and traditional forms of provision.[3] Our focus is a different and necessarily wider one. For us, the notion of an online university is useful not as a depiction of a particular type of institution, nor as a simple choice between one form of university and another, but rather as a description of a series of projects that are being implemented within universities. While there has been much written in recent years about individual ICT projects in higher education, this literature has often tended to skate over the question of how, and in what form, these projects can be established alongside those social, organizational, institutional and technical aspects already in place (an exception is Agre 2000a) – the question, in other words, of how ICTs are actually being built *into* universities. What struck us at the outset of our research was the sheer volume and nature of the work involved in constructing these virtual university projects to sit along side more conventional forms of provision. Indeed, our central term, and one that is substantially missing from much of the debate, is 'work'. While many might consider such a discussion in terms of a narrowly technological agenda, using the concepts and language from the sociology of technology, particularly the actor network approach, we maintain a wider notion, one that recognizes the heterogeneity of the effort involved. Given the way technologies like the Internet are often presented in tandem with the future of universities, we believe it useful to sketch out the nature of this work. We present two case studies, each of which discusses the tensions that arise once those building such technologies attempt to complement and, in some cases, replace the work that the established organizational and institutional structures undertake on behalf of the university.

This chapter focuses on projects and initiatives carried out in just one university, North_Campus. Our choice of institution was partly influenced by the university's commitment to the application of the Internet and other web-based technologies to higher education. From our work in other institutions, however, we did not find things to be different in kind (although maybe in degree).

The online university as mobile work

What is an online or virtual university? How might it differ from a non-virtual or traditional university? Cunningham and his collaborators, reviewing a range of 'new media'-related future scenarios for higher education, provide a useful summary of the vision of the virtual university:

> Picture a future in which students never meet a lecturer face to face in a class room, never physically visit the on-campus library; in fact, never set foot on the campus or into an institutional lecture-room or learning centre. Such is the future proposed by the virtual university scenario.
>
> (Cunningham et al. 1998: 179)

The defining feature here is principally an absence. What defines the virtual university, in this vision, is the way in which it presents a future characterized by the *lack* of physical co-presence ('never meet . . . never physically visit . . . never set foot on'). And with the need for co-presence removed, so too is the need for the specialist site of co-presence, the campus. From this point of view, then, the university is 'the university without walls'. This point cannot be taken too literally. The people who make up the university still have to be somewhere (and require the protection of walls), but what is significant is that they no longer all need to be in the *same* place. The virtual university, then, is the 'distributed university'.

What is it that makes this distribution appear possible? At one level, the answer is clear; it is information and, more specifically, communications technologies. Yet, for us, this does not get to the root of the matter. The mere presence of the communications technologies on its own does not permit the distribution of the university. For us, rather, the key point is that the technologies are used to *move* the work of the university around. Most obviously, communications technologies enable this work to be transferred between locations, linking up students, lecturers, researchers, administrators, technicians, funders, evaluators and assessors without the need for co-presence. But the virtual university also promises to redistribute work tasks in other ways. Work can be shifted around in time as well as space, with materials stored and made accessible 24 hours a day. New divisions of labour between different categories of individuals within the university become possible. Work can be shifted from staff to students, i.e. students can take on responsibility for checking and maintaining some parts of their student records, relieving administrative and academic staff of this task; administrative staff can take on tasks formerly allocated to academic staff and vice versa (see Pollock and Cornford 2000). Finally, we can talk of the possibility of a new division of labour between people and machines as computers can take on much of the laborious work of compilation, storage and distribution. The virtual university, then, is a new social, technical, temporal and spatial division of labour in higher education – it is work made mobile.

The work of making work mobile

As we have said, the mere presence of the communications technologies does not allow work to be mobile. Rather, in order to become mobile, work must be transposed into a format that is compatible with the technologies in use. In short, it must be untangled from its local constraints, stripped of its existing linkages, and then translated into information. The scale of resource required is increasingly recognized. The up-front costs of the virtual university are large, whether we are talking about administrative systems, systems to support teaching and learning, library catalogues or specialist research facilities (CVCP 2000). But what are these resources required for? On one hand, it is the hardware and software of the new systems. The technical configuration of those systems and the recoding of existing materials into a machine-readable form also constitute a portion of the work required. On the other hand, the working of such systems and software into the university demands various other activities, the type and scale of which are not easily appreciated. These range from issues to do with the identity of the university, assumptions about its role, functions and relationships, to recognizing the underlying sets of assumptions, dispositions and behaviours – the common sense of the institution, its unexamined 'organizational infrastructure' – on which these are built and depend. Typically such dependencies are difficult topics to investigate. The primary reason for this is that much of this shared common sense simply remains invisible, until, that is, something happens and we then witness how some of the most basic and taken-for-granted resources, conventions or categories of modern university life come to the fore. A secondary reason is that we simply lack the language and tools to examine how the mundane processes of rolling out new and advanced technologies interrelates with the common-sense 'doing' on which institutions like universities are based.

The notion of network building, as developed within the sociology of scientific knowledge and actor network approach, is useful here. For example, through a number of laboratory ethnographies and historical studies, Latour and his colleagues paint a picture of the scientific and technological process as one where the central actors are treated not simply as scientists or technologists but as multifaceted entrepreneurs or 'heterogeneous engineers' (Law 1994). These actors engage not only in those practices typically thought of as scientific or technological but also in a wide range of political, sociological and economic processes. In this sense, to understand just how scientific knowledge is constructed or a technology becomes a success, we must follow and observe these innovators as they attempt to enrol others (objects, buildings, people, texts, etc.) into 'networks'. Moreover, the metaphor of the network is useful for foregrounding all those typically invisible work processes, objects and actors that are essential in the construction of an enduring network (in Latour's case to describe how scientific knowledge extends itself out of the laboratory to dominate other forms of knowledge, but in our case to describe the introduction of these new technologies). In particular, we want to show how this perspective is useful when considering how new technologies have to wrestle with the inertia of those elements already in place, i.e. the existing organizational form, infrastructures and practices. As we have suggested, the actor network approach's primary focus is on change – the introduction of new networks – and it has developed a series of terms and concepts to describe this process. The radical argument of actor network theory is that it is not simply the agency of the innovator that makes a network a success, but it is the fact that this heterogeneous engineer is able to steer the agency of all the other elements that make up the network in the direction that he or she requires.[4]

Building the virtual university into the traditional university

One of the places we became interested in during our research was the Learning Development Services (LDS) department of North_Campus. In particular, we followed and observed the activities of Tom who had been working in LDS as a telematics development officer for some years. Tom's official role was to 'enrich the existing teaching and learning provision given to students through increasing the use of ICTs among academic staff'. In one of our first meetings with Tom he told us how there had recently been a number of important changes to his remit and how these had stemmed from the reorientation of North_Campus more generally. Below, he describes his current role and the way this is beginning to alter:

> What's really interesting is that there has been a massive shift really in what [my boss] and the Vice Chancellor want us to try and achieve now. My main job as Telematics Development Officer has been enrichment up until now where I have worked with a lecturer trying to put some telematics into their web materials, or move a little bit of their traditional teaching onto the web. About two months ago, [my boss] came down with a directive from above saying that she wants us to get the old print based [courses] that are working well out there in the field and convert them to run on the web, entirely telematically, so that people can log in on one of the browsers like Netscape, run it from anywhere and be completely standalone so that they can operate at a distance from the university.

This conversion of the 'old print based' courses (what Tom calls a 'conversion job') is only one facet of the planned reorientation under way:

> In the last 18 months or so, there's been another big push in the university as we've changed here again, and we're looking to try and find markets outside the university where we can deal direct with the student. So the student's a bit like an Open University student with us – we interface with them on a one-to-one basis but mediated through the technologies. So we've all been trying – several lecturers in the Computing Department, a few staff in LDS, and one or two other keen individuals dotted around the university – to come up with a model of a package that the student could reasonably be expected

to sit down in front of and plough away on their own and self-study all the way through.

During the period of our research we were able to observe examples from each of these themes. First, in terms of curriculum enrichment, there was a virtual seminar conducted as part of a photography degree course. Video-conferencing technologies were used to connect researchers and students based in the UK with researchers and students located in other parts of Europe, the idea being that they could present work and ideas to each other and receive feedback much like a traditional seminar. In terms of transferring existing print-based courses to the Internet, there was an Information Skills module that had previously been taken by over 300 first-year students every year, the aim being to familiarize them with the technologies, practices and procedures of the library. Previously run and supervised by library staff, it was to be developed into an online self-study module, which would be available anywhere on campus via the university network. (A third example, a package that would be used to attract new students from a distance, is developed in the next chapter.)

In order to understand how these projects worked out in practice we followed the progress of Tom and his team as they began to construct these new networks. Month after month we sat in on technical sessions and planning meetings as the academic material was gathered, the technology developed, and the form of these initiatives began to take shape. Staff and students willing to be part of the project rollout were identified and enrolled as participants. Yet, just several months after everything had seemingly been put in place, both projects had 'stalled'. The immediate reasons for this are varied: one of the partners pulled out of the video-conferencing project complaining of high telecommunications costs, and library staff could not be convinced that the online version of their Information Skills course was sufficiently improved to warrant its introduction in place of existing methods.

While these failures might be accounted for in a number of different ways, this is not the primary concern here.[5] Rather we are interested in these initiatives because of the way they usefully highlight the extent and nature of the work that is demanded before these new networks can be knitted into the existing arrangements within North_Campus. In the process of going online, the university has to 'rework' and rethink much of what it currently does and reconfigure its relationship with the numerous actors and entities on which it currently depends (see Agre 2000a). Moreover, it was only when attempts were made to abstract courses or activities from the campus – to make them virtual – that the necessity for, and nature of, all of this effort became visible. And with this there was the realization of the costs and complexity of seeking to compensate for the work that the various networks already in place so discretely undertake on behalf of the university. To understand these points more clearly, we need to look at each initiative in greater detail. Let us begin with the video-conferencing project.

The virtual university only partially exists

The great power and appeal of communications technologies is that they seemingly provide for the opportunity to connect places that have hitherto never been connected. The virtual seminar involved four institutions in three countries. It included active participants from the academic staff and postgraduates as well as a more 'passive' undergraduate audience. The official history of the seminar, as told by those involved in its conception, was that they simply wanted to use video-conferencing to establish connections with universities in other places; the detailed format and rationale for the project, as they saw it, would come later. The seminar ran on several occasions during the academic year and, indeed, as the project developed, a number of important outcomes became apparent. First, it was thought that, once the participants had established links with other institutions, it might then be possible to share expertise in areas where they were weak. What really excited the participants at the British university, for instance, was that the technology might allow their more practically oriented undergraduates and postgraduates access to the more theoretically oriented European academics:

> We did a pilot this year, and it was about a year in brewing it up. The [Belgian partner] suggested a module of study to follow, and then everyone threw in different papers, Bob, and Kath, and someone called Sergio over there did something for us, but also Bill wrote a short paper, and a woman from Liege University wrote a paper as well. They took it in turns to present their papers and here we have a calendar of these things [pointing to the screen]. These are the video-conference links, you know where we link up with the camera and an ISDN line, and we gave 20 minute talks, each person giving presentations, and the students from all four universities sat in and listened to those talks. There was about five minutes at the end of each talk for the students to ask genuine questions, you know, to the lecturer who had just spoken. So in a way we have got a way of sharing specialists in that subject.

It was also thought that the presentations might even be useful as 'learning material' for undergraduate students who were the audience in the seminar:

> ... that was the video conferencing bit, but the web bit is that the lecturers then put the stuff up on the web. For example, Sergio put his paper up there. The students could dip into it and read it. And then, the last bit – most important bit, I always think – is the seminar part. What they did here is that the students were allowed to go and email, quite long emails, into a giant email box that everybody else can see. So it is like a live open forum. And the students can start to follow things up. [The emails] get quite long. There were really quite considered contributions.

The compelling aspect of this story is that mundane technologies such as email and video-conferencing equipment appear to make the scenario of the online university possible; actors and institutions who never cooperated before are brought together in new alliances and affiliations to produce novel forms of higher education not previously available; work is moved from staff based in one place to those located elsewhere; and, thus, students are able to draw on expertise and knowledge from outside the walls of their own institution.

From the beginning, the seminar had been an extra module for the North_Campus students, one for which they had volunteered (in the other countries it was a core module). Such was its apparent success, however, that it was decided to make it a regular feature and include it as a compulsory aspect of the degree course. Yet, just a short time before the new academic year was about to begin, and the seminar was to run with a new set of students, we were told that there had been some difficulties and it had, therefore, been decided 'temporarily' to postpone the seminar. When we asked why this might have happened we were told that the partners in the Netherlands had pulled out because the organization allowing them to use a video-conferencing suite had decided to charge them the equivalent of £50 an hour to use it.

While we do not discount this financial story (although the small sums of money involved make us doubt its adequacy), we want to add a further aspect to this. Typically, we understand technologies in terms of what they might afford. Thus it could be suggested that it was the connections afforded by the video-conferencing equipment and email that initially allowed the project to get off the ground, and since other universities with the same technology were assumed to have a similar interest in being connected, the project began to flourish. Yet, as already mentioned, the virtual seminar was entirely technology led – based simply on a desire to use video-conferencing within the university. And, as Latour and others remind us, the work of innovation involves not simply a requirement to contend oneself with the 'technological' specifics of the artefact but also, and just as importantly, the simultaneous construction of other (political, sociological and economic) ties. This was crucial if the project was to extend its influence within the wider networks of the university. Among other things, this might be the establishment of an idea or a concept that can link the virtual seminar to the wider institutional goals (its educational aims and mission, and the role that technology might play in this). In other words, the seminar lacked a context into which it could be inserted. Presumably, the goal of connection appeared self-evidently a 'good' and 'necessary' thing without further need of elaboration.

Perhaps it was no surprise, then, that once the seminar had to jump this first minor financial hurdle, the collaborators in the other universities found it was simply unable to. The seminar had no context or other connections to draw upon.[6] Tom describes how, in a meeting with the European partners to discuss the merits of the seminar and the potential for collaboration

with other universities, the partners had decided, in the context of commit-
ments to existing education methods, that the seminar 'wasn't worthwhile'.
Interestingly, shortly after this meeting, Tom's own institution also began to
question the benefits of financing further video-conferencing projects. Tom
again: 'It's funny, at the same time [as the European partners pulled out of
the project], in my university I've always had a £3,000 budget to spend on
anyone who wants to do video-conferencing from my room, and my budget
has been cut on that as well.' Indeed, as far as Tom is concerned, just a
couple of months after the technology had seemingly brought all these
actors together into a network, video-conferencing within his university had
'come and gone'.

In summary, we have discussed what might be described as a failure to
extend a network; the seminar was not fully integrated into the university
and this lack of context or limited means of connection meant that the
project was conceived of and remained simply a 'technical project'. For the
actor network approach, a technology becomes a success only when a sufficient network has been built for it. Indeed, as Rudinow Saetnan (1991)
points out, without such connections a technology can be said to only
'partially exist'. Finding a way of conceiving of these virtual projects appears
also as an issue in our second case study, the Information Skills course, to
which we now turn.

What is a course?

New technologies often demand the rethinking and reworking of the most
basic and essential concepts (Kiesler and Sproull 1987). The idea behind
the Information Skills course was to take 'old print based material' which
was 'working well out there in the field' and convert this to run on the web.
The course could therefore be completely 'standalone and accessible at a
distance from the university'. What became apparent while carrying out this
'conversion job', however, was the extent to which a tension was created in
the existing organizational arrangements within North_Campus. Seemingly,
those established concepts and practices which were in place were not
capable of supporting the role that these advanced technologies asked of
them.

Let us elaborate what this means through a description of one particular
meeting where Tom and Sonia, a programmer from LDS, are demonstrat-
ing the new online version of the Information Skills course to one of the
assistant directors of the library, Helen. Helen is responsible for running
the existing course and it is she who will decide if the online version will get
the go-ahead. While we are waiting for Helen to arrive, Sonia describes how
she is nervous about the forthcoming meeting. She has spent the summer
turning the Information Skills material into something that can be put on
the web and now she has reached the most crucial stage: the coding work
is complete and she and Tom are ready to demonstrate it to Helen. Her

nervousness rests on the fact that while translating the course she has made some necessary modifications to its format. Until recently, Helen had appeared supportive of the idea. In recent weeks, however, she has been less forthcoming, both in terms of providing more information about the course and in her attitude and interest.

Towards the end of the demonstration Helen concludes that she likes the package but that she is not sure how to proceed with it. Tom's suggestion is to test the package with some of her students over the next few weeks. However, she is not convinced that this is how it should be taken forward: as she understands it, no trial could possibly occur until the university had validated the course. What follows is a lengthy discussion about the need for validation. Sonia is convinced that there is no need to put the package through the validation process as, despite her modifications, she believes it is in essence the 'same course'. Helen disagrees: anything that has 'substantial modifications' has to be re-evaluated. The discussion whether or not the course is the same or different goes on for some time. Indeed, at some points we observed how there was even some ambiguity about what a course, one of the most taken-for-granted categories of the university, actually was: is it a traditional course, a traditional course just put onto the web, or is it something completely new?

The problem appeared to be that the project team were not willing to describe the course in *too novel* terms for fear that the online version's genesis from the original Information Skills module would be completely disregarded. It is not simply that, if seen to be completely new, the course will have to be revalidated, but that the processes and procedures for validating an online course will themselves have to be created and put in place. At the same time, however, if they use a concept that is too fully rooted to the conventional conception of the course, then they run the risk of their work never being adopted, as the team believed the library staff would not go to the effort of implementing something that was simply an online version of what they are teaching now. Thus, the project team attempt to deploy a notion of a course that is *simultaneously* old and new: it is both a traditional course and it is a new virtual university course.

Finally, the meeting breaks up and Tom appears disappointed. It had not gone as he has planned. He is particularly upset that Helen might want to have the course revalidated, telling us that in all previous dealings he had managed to avoid dealing with the 'centre' and that he had hoped to do the same this time around as well.[7] Now it will mean much more work for his team and, probably, he thinks, the module will never be launched. Such confrontations we found during our research were commonplace.

Conclusion

What is particular about our account of why these projects 'stalled'? Three reasons are conventionally put forward for the failure of such initiatives: the technology does not work (or does not work as expected); staff, in particular teaching staff, actively or passively resist the introduction of the technology which threatens their autonomy (for example, by removing their control of course construction and use); and, finally, that the costs of such courses are simply too high, at least when they are not spread across large numbers of learners. There is, of course, something in each of these analyses. We would argue, however, that each of these arguments is superficial. In none of the cases we looked at did the technology fail. Further, there was no overt staff resistance to the introduction of the courses. On the contrary, all the teaching staff involved were, somewhat to our surprise, more or less keen on the use of the technology, and where there was criticism, this was offered in a constructive manner. Finally, while the issue of costs did emerge frequently in each of the cases, it was the costs of the work of (re)configuring the institution, rather than those of the technology, that eventually emerged as significant.

What we would argue, then, is that each of these three reasons can be seen as simply the surface manifestation of an underlying tension between the old and the new: between established technological configurations and the new context of higher education in which they are deployed; between the engagement of staff in the established networks of the university and the possibilities of the new, and more technologically mediated, networks of the 'online' university; and, finally, the tension between the conventionally accounted costs of course construction and the revealed costs of (re) creating the context in which virtual courses can survive (including the problems of accounting for these).

Returning to the quotation with which we began this chapter, the underlying problem in each case is the sheer volume and complexity of the work required to configure the multiple actors – people, machines, objects, texts, and money – all of which are already enrolled more or less consciously in existing networks.

What form of university is emerging in the light of the increasing applications of new ICTs? On the one hand, it is unlikely that there will be an absolute transformation of the university: its core role and functions cannot simply be shifted online overnight; physical places like campuses are increasingly relevant; and there is little evidence to suggest that learners find fully online courses (Hara and Kling 2000) or electronic study resources (Stephens 1999) wholly appropriate to their needs. On the other hand, staff and students are increasingly reliant on information systems, the Internet, and other online technologies to conduct their everyday routines. Indeed, the nature of academic work is changing as scholars find themselves using more technology, and not only within scientific and technological fields (Star and Ruhleder 1996): communication between these scholarly communities is increasingly shaped by the possibilities (and limitations) afforded by email (Walsh and Bayma 1996); new undergraduates increasingly want to complete registration procedures online rather than wait in line at a desk, and so on.

The picture we painted at North_Campus is, then, just as equivocal. Despite the early phase where the projects appeared to flourish, albeit within the close confines of the team and allied groups (what Law and Callon (1995) have called a 'negotiation space'), once attempts were made to extend these networks into the university or, as in the case of the virtual seminar, where the institution enters the space of the project, each 'stalled'. In essence, the initiatives demanded the rethinking and reworking of relations between a wide-ranging set of actors and entities, many of which were well beyond the imagined scope of basic technologies. The abstraction and distribution of courses and activities from the campus creates not only obvious divisions of labour between staff, students and objects, as well as places, but also problems of coordination; through the virtual seminar we saw the bringing together of a wide range of actors and entities across a number of large organizations with no procedures for interacting other than those mediated through the technology. Attempts to introduce online modules also brought about shifts in boundaries too; for instance, between the new and the old (was the course the same, just put onto a computer, or something completely new?). These kinds of shifts inevitably have consequences elsewhere, which, while often mundane, slow and complicate the whole process of putting the university online. For instance, there were no procedures for validating online courses within North_Campus and therefore these had to be built. Overall, for Tom and his team, this meant that it was difficult to enrol (or to keep enrolled) all of those aspects of the university necessary to make the projects work.

Crucial to whichever form(s) of university that may emerge is the 'work' of building the virtual university *into* the traditional university. Pivotal to this has been the effort of the project team and the multifaceted or 'intermediation' role they have played as they have grappled with the various technologies, sociologies, economics, politics and materialities of campus life. We say intermediation role because the team are, like Janus, attempting to face different directions at the same time (Latour 1987). They are trying to build the virtual university from within the constraints and limitations of the traditional university and the issue for them is whether to continue to work with, and try to fit these new online courses and seminars into, existing concepts, arrangements and infrastructures, or to begin to call into being new and different ones. Such work – this continual movement back and forth between the existing institution and the (often mismatched) requirements of the new projects – is slow, complex and prone to failure. This is because the university, like most institutions, has a large number of networks, infrastructures and routines that are not easily recognized or changed (cf. Agre 2000b). The problem that Tom and his team face, described from the point of view of organizational economics, could thus be seen as a choice between exploring new technology mediated possibilities and the exploitation of old certainties (cf. March 1989). In other words, the issue for universities as they face the challenges brought about by ICTs is to choose which aspects of their existing institution they should continue to exploit and which of the promises of the new technologies they should begin to explore.

Notes

1. For instance, in a recent and widely circulated letter by the Higher Education Funding Council for England (HEFCE) the dangers of such 'virtual and corporate universities' eating into the UK higher education market were spelt out. The letter invites universities to respond to this threat by contributing to a new 'e-University' project that will challenge these new entrants. The document can be found on HEFCE's website: http://www.hefce.ac.uk/Pubs/CircLets/2000/cl104_00.htm
2. See, for instance, some of the projects mentioned in a special issue of *Futures*, 30(7), 1998, in the special issue of *Information, Communication and Society*, 30(4), 2000, or in *Minerva*, 39(1), 2001.
3. Several of the advocates have already been mentioned in the introduction. Some of the critics include David Noble (1998) and Langdon Winner (1998).
4. Callon's (1986b) notion of radical symmetry is that no one element (human or non-human) in a network is assumed to be more important than any other; they all, methodologically at least, have equal status.
5. We certainly do not want to be critical of the staff in the Learning Development Services department who, despite limited resources, often showed remarkable ingenuity and resourcefulness in their work.
6. For instance, see Green and Harvey's (1999) account of the different senses of 'connection' as it is typically discussed by technology advocates and, in contrast, how it might be understood elsewhere (as in anthropology or actor network theory). The upshot of their argument is that whereas technology can be effective at maintaining existing connections or relations between actors it is less good at building new ones. See also Brown and Duguid (2000: ch. 8), where a similar argument is made.
7. Of course, what Tom is referring to as the 'centre' is, among other things, the tradition within universities of 'rule by committee'. For a good description of the workings of the committee system, see Lockwood and Davies (1985).

4

The Campus
and the Online University

The way forward is not to look ahead, but to look around.

(Brown and Duguid 2000: 8)

Introduction

It may appear strange to have a whole chapter of a book on virtual universities given over to the subject of the university campus. Surely, one may suggest, the whole point of online or distributed education, its appeal to students, its very rationale, is to extend learning opportunities beyond the confines of, perhaps even to transcend, the university campus. Further, one may argue, The Open University and similar institutions around the world have proved that higher education can do without the encumbrance of the campus. Communication between staff, students and administrators can be undertaken by telephone, post and email.

Yet peer closer and the campus refuses to quite disappear. The Open University has both a significant campus of it own in Milton Keynes, Buckinghamshire, for staff, researchers and postgraduate students – what we might think of as 'the campus as back office' – and makes extensive use of the facilities of other universities for its summer schools. In this chapter we want to explore the role of the campus in online education. We want to show how the campus – or more generally the collocation of learners and teachers – refuses to lie down and die. More specifically, we want to show some of the subtle and powerful, if often taken-for-granted, ways in which the campus *works* to support higher education. This is not say that a campus is necessary to effective education or that distributed education is in some sense inferior to a campus-based education. They are simply different. What is important, however, is that those seeking to develop distributed education understand the support that a campus setting gives the education process and are prepared for the need to find new ways of providing that support in a distributed education context.

The virtual university and the campus-as-constraint

Around the world, both new and existing higher educational institutions are seeking to harness the capacities of information and communications technologies (ICTs) to build 'virtual' or online universities. This signifies a seeming decrease in importance of the traditional campus-based university as degree courses are increasingly being delivered and assessed over the Internet. Although the specific features of the various projects under way may vary widely, they share a core vision, a notion of distributed learning in which geographical distance is fetishized as that-which-is-to-be-overcome, a constraint which we can now transcend. Abeles, for instance, is one of many authors who sees in ICTs the promise of freeing knowledge from the confines of the campus:

> knowledge, which was once captured in the cloistered halls and libraries of academia, in a wired world, is immediately made available. Similarly students who once travelled great distances to listen to lectures of scholars, can now access this knowledge via the world of the Internet.
>
> (Abeles 1998: 606)

Here we have a description of the virtual university in terms of a disruption of the traditional understanding of how knowledge is positioned in space and time: knowledge once contained within the physical and temporal constraints of the university campus is now, as a result of the Internet, available anywhere and at any time. As we have argued in Chapter 3, the defining feature of the wholly online university is principally that of absence. The essence of the virtual university, in this vision, is the way in which it presents a future characterized by the *lack* of physical co-presence ('never meet . . . never physically visit . . . never set foot on' – Cunningham *et al.* 1998: 179). And with the need for co-presence removed, it is often argued, so too is the need for the specialist site of co-presence, the conventional university campus with its classrooms, library, laboratories, lecture rooms and learning centres.

In this 'virtual' university scenario there is still, of course, a kind of coming together of students, teachers and texts, but it is a 'virtual' coming together, mediated by modern digital communications networks, rather than one facilitated by the concrete physical presence of the campus. With no face-to-face meetings, with no need to access physical resources such as books, the physical context for such coming together of things and bodies becomes redundant. From the perspective of this vision of the virtual university, then, the conventional campus is seen as, at best, an anachronism. At worst is seen as a constraint on the reach of the institution and a drain on its resources. The dominant spatial form of higher education as we have known it since the Middle Ages is transcended.

The university-level, or 'higher', education has seen a gradual geographical extension since its origins in Bologna and Paris in the Middle Ages. And as it has become more widely spread (or even perhaps distributed?) it has undergone a wide range of transformations (for example, secularization, extension of the curriculum beyond the liberal arts and professions to take in the sciences and technology, the incorporation of research as a core university mission, the admission of women, and so on). Most dramatically, perhaps, there has been the expansion in the number of institutions that call themselves universities, and, more recently, the expansion in the proportion of the population that, at some point in their lives, will experience a 'university education'. Through these many changes, both revolutionary and evolutionary, however, the dominant spatial form of the university – the campus – has been, if not unchanging, a relative constant. Throughout its history, the majority of people with a university education have 'gone to' a university, and they have gone to it with others.

Let us be clear: there certainly have been institutions which have successfully laid claim to the title of 'university' and which have not relied, or not relied totally, on the traditional campus (The Open University to name but one); and we are well aware of the significant differences between different kinds of campus from the collegiate sprawl of Oxford or Cambridge, through the compact city centre redbricks of a Leeds, Sheffield or Manchester, to the secluded edge-of-city campuses of the 1960s such as Lancaster or Sussex. There are even 'multi-campus' universities (such as those of London or California). Nevertheless, all of these manifestations call themselves, and are recognized as, university campuses.

The virtual university vision of distributed higher education still has a spatial form, of course – the irreducibly physical components of the educational experience, the bodies of students and some form of shelter for them, the technologies required to display texts and images, the networks of wires, fibres and switches which connect them, still have to exist in some definite space (although they may be increasingly mobile). What is significant, however, is that these various elements can be very widely *distributed* in space, tied together by information technology. These elements cannot be quite anywhere – there are enough inequalities in the quality and costs of the necessary network infrastructures to ensure that, for much of the population of the world and in many places, this scenario is infeasible. But for a large, and growing, portion of the world's population, there are no substantial *technical* barriers to such a vision.

But let us examine this scenario more closely. As we argued above, to be able to distribute the elements of learning in this way requires the coordinating and communicating power of digital network technologies to enable texts sounds and images – in short, information – to be communicated and shared in a timely fashion. The reliance on these technologies, and the kinds of information that they can handle, promotes a strong notion of the learning experience in terms of 'information', its creation or assembly, storage, transmission, sharing and processing. Higher education, then, comes to be seen almost exclusively in terms of *information* (see Chapter 5).

Now, the modern(ist) concept of information that lies at the heart of the vision of a virtual university carries with it an implicit (anti)geography.

Theodore Porter, for example, writing on the role of information in social organization, has pointed towards the close linkage between information as a social category and questions of space and scale:

> the creation and use of information needs to be understood first of all as a problem of space and of scale, of getting beyond what is local, personal or intimate and creating knowledge that is, so far as possible, neutral and well standardized . . . knowledge detached from the skills and close acquaintanceships that flourish in local sites.
>
> (1994: 217)

'The ideal', he suggests, 'is to go beyond perspective, to turn a view from somewhere into a "view from nowhere"' (ibid.: 229). Note how closely this 'view from nowhere' mirrors the promise which ICTs hold for the university of permitting an escape from ('getting beyond') the confines of the campus ('local sites'), and entry into a global higher education market – the possibility of being present everywhere. However, Porter also contrasts 'a world of information', understood as 'a world of standardized objects and neutralized subjects', with a 'local site where skill and intimate familiarity with people and things provide the most promising route to success' (Porter 1994: 221; cf. Boden and Molotch 1994).

This kind of contrast between an informational view of higher education, characteristic of the online or virtual university discourse, and other kinds of knowledge, those more rooted in place, echoes many critiques of the virtual university. For example, Newman and Johnson identify the virtual university as being based on a 'naïve sociology' which 'ignores the role of apprenticeship and implicit craft knowledge in the generation of technical progress and scientific discovery' (Newman and Johnson 1999: 80), the role of face-to-face interaction and group socialization. Other writers reinforce these latter points, building on notions of 'the hidden curriculum' and of a university education as being a 'rite of passage'. Kumar, for example, argues that:

> Nowhere else, and at no other time in their lives, irrespective of age, will students encounter each other with so much time and so many resources to do so much, unconstrained by the requirements of job or family. The university is indeed a *place*, a physical space with buildings and grounds that exist to facilitate the pursuits of students and teachers.
>
> (1997: 32, italics in original)

The informational view of the university, then, has not gone unchallenged, the significance of place and co-presence for the wider higher educational experience has been asserted. In the next section, however, we want to delve deeper into some of the ways in which the campus, as the place of higher education par excellence, reasserts itself, without recourse to these wider arguments. In order to do this we need some kind of analytical framework within which we can view the process of development of distance education.

Creating distance education as the assemblage of actor networks

How can we think about distributed education in a new way? Here we return to the notion of actor networks as one way of doing this. Through studies of the construction of scientific and technical knowledge, we have learnt to recognize more of the real work involved in the process of building scientific facts or in the production of technological systems. Traditionally we have understood the invention and diffusion of important and transformational scientific theories and technologies (for instance, the process of pasteurization, the invention of the electric light or the telegraph, and so on) in narrow and simplistic terms. The result has been that the history of science and technology has been told in a certain way, often from the viewpoint of certain heroic human actors.

More recent work, however, has sought to challenge this view, seeing science and technology as a matter of network-building or system-building where various elements are brought together or 'enrolled' into an assemblage which is capable of 'acting as one' (see, for instance Bruno Latour's analysis of Pasteur in *The Pasteurization of France* (1988a), or Thomas Hughes' description of Edison in *Networks of Power* (1983)). What the metaphor of the network allows is the foregrounding of all the work, processes, objects and actors that are essential to understanding how entities such as the campus endure but which typically remain invisible.

Many conceptualizations of the virtual university are based on an implicit analysis of education as an informational process, one concerned with the movement of information from one place to another. This point of view is, for example, well illustrated by the widespread use of terms such as 'course delivery'. Using concepts from actor network theory, we can attempt to move away from this narrow informational view of learning and theorize these attempts to build distance education as a form of heterogeneous engineering – the binding together of various elements (typically people, texts, objects and machines), all of which can be regarded as actors. From this wider point of view, we can turn our attention to the role of the campus – itself a complex assemblage of people, texts, objects and machines, brought within spatial scale of everyday life and coordinated in time – in higher education.

To exemplify what is meant here, we might start from Edward Thompson's (1980) classic text, *Writing by Candlelight*. Written at the time of a miners' strike in the UK, Thompson describes how, when we throw a switch to turn on an electric light we do not generally think about the work of those who laboured to dig out the coal, or pump the oil or gas, work that is necessary to make the connection between throwing the switch and the light coming on. From an actor network perspective, however, we would highlight not only the labouring bodies of the workers but also the huge network of wires, switches, fuses, transformers, power stations, gas and oil drilling rigs, tankers and lorries; the shadow control networks and monitoring systems;

the customer billing systems and international commodity exchanges; the regulatory texts and bodies that control standards and prices; the huge volumes of technical and financial documentation necessary to run these systems; and, finally, the disciplined consumers who both 'plug in' and pay for the benefits of doing so.

Of course, this huge network will only become visible to most when some part of it begins to break down (i.e. when throwing the switch fails to turn on the light). In Thompson's example, the cause of the breakdown was the withdrawal of labour by the miners. However, from an actor network perspective, not only people, but any of the elements in the network could be the cause of the breakdown – for example, a blown fuse or light bulb, a power line that has blown down in a gale, etc.[1] In short, all of these elements have to *work* together for the light to respond to the switch. Even though what it means to work is very different for a miner, a wire and a light bulb, they can all be seen as performing, or not performing, their role in the context of the network as a whole. In other words, no one element (human or non-human) is assumed, *a priori*, to be more important than any other; they all, methodologically at least, have equal status. What is valuable for us about this perspective is that it enables us to move away from an analysis of learning solely in terms of its informational *content* and to introduce a concern for the real effects that the *forms* which that content comes in, make. Finally, it also enables us to rethink what a campus is, to extend the notion of the campus from an exclusive focus on the everyday convergence of human actors in time and space and to treat seriously the physical nature of the campus, its buildings, laboratories, library, classrooms, quadrangles, halls of residence, and so on, and to acknowledge the work that they perform (or fail to perform).

Further useful concepts from the actor network approach are those of 'immutable mobiles' and 'action at a distance'. Developed from early ethnographic studies of 'science in action' (Latour 1987), these concepts attempted to redescribe science as a literary and interpretative activity, where scientific facts are constructed, circulated and evaluated as written statements. The production of such literary devices – entities such as charts, diagrams, figures, papers, and so on – has, as Latour suggests, always been a central feature of scientific activity. For instance, academic papers are highly portable and retain their form and shape while being moved around, and they can be circulated and read in new places. In other words, these immutable mobiles can act at a distance from their place of production: others can both evaluate and act on the findings reported in a new paper. This immutability and mobility, Latour suggests, is one of the reasons that scientific knowledge has dominated other forms of knowledge.

If this set of ideas can be applied to science, then they can also be applied to our discussion of distributed education. The most fundamentally educational technologies – textbooks, for example – are of course centrally concerned with making learning materials both relatively immutable and portable in time and space. With the circulation of textbooks, the author no longer needs to be co-present with the student, as the text itself acts on his or her behalf, albeit at a distance.

How does all of this relate to questions of distance education and the role of the campus in distance education? First, we can describe the construction of distance education courses in terms of the construction of an actor network – the painstaking piecing together of people (lecturers, authors, technicians, librarians, graphic artists, publishers, assessment experts, administrators, students, etc.), machines and other physical items (computers, telecommunications networks, offices, etc.), texts (textbooks, course lists, examination papers and assessment forms, etc.), and, of course, money (budgets, accounts, direct debits, etc.). Second, the virtual university as a project has the goal of transcending the constraints of the campus. But, we ask, to what extent is the campus a constraint? If you want to know the role that the campus has in the existing actor networks of the university, simply imagine the extra work that would be necessary if that entity was not present. Once we begin to embrace the complexity that the actor network approach affords, might we think of the campus as other than a constraint, perhaps even a resource?

The campus as a resourceful constraint

To work towards a better understanding, we want to step back from the notion of the actor network for a moment and draw on Wenger and Lave's notion of a 'community of practice' (Wenger 1998) and to contrast this with what we feel is the dominant process-oriented or flow-oriented view of distributed learning.

The current explosion of interest in, and experimentation with, distributed learning has come about in a wider context strongly shaped by process-oriented views of socio-technical systems. The paradigmatic version of this view is the popular management notion of business process re-engineering, or BPR. From a BPR perspective, an organization can be broken down into, and is understood in terms of, its core value-adding processes. The aim of the organization should be to make these processes as lean and as efficient as possible. The stress in BPR, then, is on the *flow* of work, activities and documents through the organization. Re-engineering is focused on making these pathways *through* the organization as smooth and as speedy as possible. The application of ICTs to the task of simplifying and speeding up these 'document flows', 'workflows' or 'act flows' has become a central component of the 're-engineering revolution' which has in turn shaped the thinking and practices of technology design companies.

In practice, then, the stress in BPR is on converting the outputs of one process quickly and effectively into the inputs for the next process. Far less attention, however, is given to how work is actually undertaken within each process, and workers are seen primarily in the context of the chain of processes in which they are inserted, a 'longitudinal' view.

Wenger and Lave's notion of a community of practice stands in strong contrast to this process-oriented view. For Wenger, the process-oriented view, which sees the worker only in the context of the linkages running longitudinally through the organization, misses out on important lateral relationships. In Wenger's classic study of clerks handling medical insurance claims forms, the managers of the insurance company saw the work of the clerks almost exclusively in terms of their insertion within the longitudinal business process. Their work and reward structures were constructed in terms of how effectively they processed the constant stream of medical claims forms which flowed into and out of the office (did they meet 'production'?). Wenger's ethnographic research with these claims processors, by contrast, revealed the extent to which their work was supported and facilitated by the 'lateral' interaction among the claims processors, interaction that was all but invisible to the managers. Jointly, the claims processors had developed a body of knowledge that enabled them to process the forms drawing on shared knowledge, heuristics and precedents. Wenger goes on to theorize this lateral interaction in terms of the notion of a 'community of practice' (see Wenger 1998).

Brown and Duguid's (2000) recent work has usefully developed Wenger's insight and helps us to challenge the view of the campus as merely a constraint. This notion, we suggest, relies on a specific and partial perspective on (higher) education which privileges the kind of longitudinal-, process- or information-oriented understanding of universities, and fails to acknowledge adequately the importance of lateral linkages between individuals engaged in the same (kind of) task.

Brown and Duguid provide a useful example, drawn from the Xerox Corporation (for whom Brown works) of Xerox copier machine repair engineers. Xerox's management understood the work process of these engineers as being in essence concerned with the interpretation of the error messages produced by machines, the interrogation of technical manuals concerning each type of photocopier and the application of the recommended solution. The engineers were seen by management as primarily working in the context of these flows of information, each independently linked to the company's knowledge base via the (centrally determined) error messages and the (centrally produced) technical manuals. The view of the engineers' work was in the context of the officially prescribed *process*.

Following an ethnographic study of the engineers in one US city, it became apparent that this was far from the case. In *practice*, the engineers were meeting together, before starting work, for breakfast. At these breakfast sessions they swapped a vast store of practical knowledge about fixing photocopiers. What is more, particular engineers became acknowledged experts, and were called up by other engineers to help fix particularly difficult problems. In fact, then, far from the individualized relationship between the engineer and the corporation, mediated via the standardized error messages and technical manuals, there was an elaborate and continually reconstructed knowledge-pool built up by the engineers and on which they all freely drew to get the job done. It was only by closely examining the actual practice of the engineers that this knowledge pool was revealed.

While Brown and Duguid's work is in essence concerned with these human or social linkages, we can, drawing on the points from actor network theory made above, extend this perspective to incorporate not only the lateral social networks – that is, networks of human beings – involved in learning but also other 'actors' (in the actor network sense) – buildings, spaces, machines, and objects – which act to facilitate and support the learning process. From this perspective, the work which the campus undertakes for the university, the subtle ways in which it supports the processes of learning and research, become apparent and its 'submerged resourcefulness' (Brown and Duguid 2000: 244) is revealed. We illustrate the argument by drawing on our fieldwork at two UK universities.

Assessing assessment

As a first example we will take the creation of an online course, based on an existing course taught in the conventional manner at one of the universities which we have studied. The aim of the course development team is to provide a course which can be taken by students on the other side of the world, accessing materials and tutors via the web, email and real-time conferencing. One of the many issues that arises during the process of course construction concerns the assessment and accreditation of the students. In the conventional mode of delivery of this course, students are assessed by an unseen, sit-down examination, undertaken simultaneously with the other students taking the course in a large examination hall. This all appears natural and unproblematic in the context of the university campus. The course team is keen to make as few changes in the course as possible, in part to save time and in part because substantial changes would require the course to be revalidated, a time-consuming procedure.

In the distributed mode, however, problems arise. How are the students to be assessed? There is, of course, no problem in transferring the examination paper to the web, thus providing access to the students. This transfer can be delayed until a given moment so that the paper remains 'unseen' (although this raises problems for students in different parts of the world – is it fair if some students take the examination in the afternoon while others take it in the middle of the night?). More problematic, but still technically possible, the students' examination answers can be emailed or electronically transferred to the tutors for marking (although time delays in the transfer of materials over the Internet mean that it is less easy to ensure that all students enjoy the same time to complete the examination). A further difficulty arises when the notion of the identity of the student emerges – how does the course team know that the student's responses are really those of the student and not those of someone else? How can they control for 'real-time plagiarism' in which a student copies from model answers posted on the web? In the campus situation, there is relatively little direct checking of the student's identity in the examination hall; indeed, the staff undertaking the exam invigilation may not even be from the same faculty as the student. There is, in practice, little to stop a student paying someone to sit their exam for them. Nevertheless, the physical collocation with other students from the course provides enough of an ordinary, everyday level of surveillance to discourage such behaviour. In the distributed scenario, without such peer surveillance, the course team is worried that plagiarism or forms of cheating based on impersonation, will be unconstrained.

How can the checks on plagiarism and impersonation which the campus situation so elegantly and discreetly provides be replicated in cyberspace. The discussion goes in a number of directions. One set of possibilities that is explored is in essence reliant on using more technology to plug the gap. Increasingly baroque potential technologies are invoked. Various forms of identification and authentication can be used, from simple passwords to, at least in theory, biometrics (technologies for recognizing unique biological features such as fingerprints and the iris patterns in the eye). All of these add to the cost and complexity of the course, without actually solving the problem. An alternative solution is to recreate the examination environment nearer the students. The university in question is working with a number of partner institutions in the countries in which the course is to be marketed and these institutions could provide the examination halls and invigilation. Here the campus as a physical setting for collocation of the examination candidates has been recreated, but on a distributed basis. Again, the costs and complexity of the course look set to balloon as the team contemplates the task of booking examination space, distributing examination papers and ensuring that all students on this distributed course can travel to a suitable partner institution. And again, if the students have not been in contact before the examination, the peer surveillance that works so effectively in the residential campus setting cannot be relied on.

The final option, and the one which eventually is pursued, is to change the mode of assessment for the course. This too is time consuming, given that the course may well need revalidation. Of course, there are many good arguments for abandoning traditional three-hour, unseen examinations sat in a large hall – and many of them were rehearsed here. However, these arguments are made after the decision to change the mode of assessment has been made, not before. While the shift to a distributed mode for the course certainly does open up some new possibilities, it is also important to note how it closes down other options – specifically here the traditional unseen three-hour examination. What is being revealed is the way in which the campus, understood as the collocation of the students and staff in time and space, quietly and unobtrusively facilitates a particular form of assessment. With the shift to a distributed mode, this form of assessment, although still possible, becomes far more technically complex and costly.

The Cyber Culture course is too virtual

Our second example of the work which campus performs concerns the development of a module on cyber culture by the Learning Development Services (LDS) team at North_Campus that we met in Chapter 3. Here, we witness the demand for various forms of boundary or 'bridging' work between the universities as they are now and the idea of a future institution. In some respects, the Cyber Culture module is the most interesting we observed as it comes closest to what is most commonly thought of as a truly virtual university: it was a completely new course that was intended to take North_Campus in a very different direction by targeting new groups of students – those outside the institution. The idea behind this course, as described by Tom, the telematics development officer charged with developing the course, was that his department should become a 'little Open University' that would be able to transact directly with its students through technological means.

As well as being a package to be sold on the Internet, the course was also to become a compulsory module on the European Studies degree programme, one taken by traditional campus-based students. Tom described the logic behind this as being that the LDS team wanted to encourage staff in other departments to become similarly involved and develop their own such online courses; and, thus, as Tom saw it, the Cyber Culture module would serve as a useful device for enrolling other members of staff. Yet, before the module can work to enlist others, it must first enrol the students. Here the team saw a potential problem: how might students accustomed to more traditional forms of teaching and learning react to a fully online course? Tom's experience of similar developments had led him to believe that students could be sometimes sceptical of such developments (the nature of which is discussed below), and as a way of alleviating this, right from the outset, Tom and his team had spent a lot of time reworking the course with these users in mind. The basic problem, as Tom saw it, was that the Cyber Culture module in its existing form was too virtual for these particular students. Indeed, the extent to which he considers this a serious issue can be seen from the following conversation where, meeting with two of the university's graphic designers, he is discussing the design of some printed material that might be incorporated into the Cyber Culture module.

> In terms of a fully online course, it will never happen. We will never go electronic. So, we have come to this kind of moment when we feel that we have to try and market – sort of market in inverted commas, but really market without the inverted commas – these materials. Internally for ourselves we have got to persuade students – I think that is the best word, it's not too strong a word – persuade students that this is a good route to choose while there is still a choice between using the printed versions and the web versions.

To gain access to the online course, the procedure is simply to issue each student with a World Wide Web address (URL), a user name and a password. However, for the project team, the fear was that a simple slip of paper sent to the student, or an email, with the necessary information to access the course would not be adequate because it would fail to effectively stand in for the work which the team and the institution had put into developing and running the course. This, it was feared, would lead the students to undervalue both the course itself and North_Campus's role in creating it. The issues, then, as Tom sees them, are persuading students of the benefits of these forms of technology and of further developing the package with this relationship in mind. Considerable effort was therefore put into finding a suitable way of making this wholly immaterial (virtual) course distinct and significant for its potential users.

The outcome of this effort was the creation of an elaborately packaged floppy disk that prominently displayed the university's logo in order to establish firmly the provenance of the course. The exact problem, as Tom sees it, is as follows:

> It's so difficult you see, because [the online courses] don't exist. I can't bring any to show you. And that is what we want the print [material] to do . . . to turn them into 'things', and that is why we slipped back to this idea of at least giving them a diskette for the first one, and then we can have students coming along to LDS and we can give them a disk out over the table, over our reception desk.

In short, the success of the virtual course becomes reliant on a functionally redundant physical token – the packaged floppy disk.

This leads us to a more general point about the nature of the online university and its relation to the campus. In common with many commentators, and indeed many of those involved in the initiatives that we studied, we began our research with the notion of the traditional place of the university – the campus – as a barrier, as something to be overcome with the aid of ICTs. Indeed, this appears more generally as a powerful trend within the discourse of virtuality. We did not, of course, suppose this represented a total escape from the constraints of geography, but rather that the university could only escape a particular spatial configuration by instituting another: to paraphrase Harvey (1987), this would be annihilating space and time through a new 'spatial fix'. Thus, we assumed that although the university could become 'disembedded' from the campus, it could only do so by becoming re-embedded in some other configuration of places.

Over the period of the research, however, we moved increasingly away from this image of disembedding and re-embedding as we were made increasingly aware of the ways in which place – the physical world of the campus – far from being simply a constraint on the activities of the university and its staff and students, performed a number of important, if unacknowledged, functions for them; it is what Agre (2000b) has described as a 'meta-place' that provides all the other places of the university with a common administrative apparatus, physical plant, and, as we have suggested, a symbolic and material resource. It is only after attempts were made to abstract a course from the campus that these roles become visible, and with this an awareness of the complexity of seeking to replace the work that the campus so discreetly undertakes.

Finally, it can be seen how the effort of substituting the work of the campus turns on its head the assumption that universities, as they take up and use more and more ICTs, will become virtual. Rather, much of the effort of building these components into the university is concerned with giving them a greater sense of material presence (cf. Wakeford 1999). Tom again: 'It is a hard move, you know moving from giving away books to, you know, giving away nothing. So, it is like this: hopefully the print will carry that through, give it that sort of solidity and life.' Unable to rely on the sheer physical presence of the campus to symbolize the university to the distance students, elaborate substitutes had to be constructed.

Conclusion

Why did the distance learning course developers that we studied seem so often to bump into the kinds of situation described above? With these two examples we have tried to show some of the work that the campus performs in conventional education – the role of mutual surveillance and the symbolic role of the campus – and to show the additional work that has to be undertaken to replace these functions in the move to effective distributed education.

What we want to draw from Wenger's work is this focus on the lateral interactions. In many of the examples of development of distributed education that we studied, the developers initially focused strongly on the process perspective, the (computer- and Internet-supported) flow of documents, activities and work from teacher to learner and back again. What was given much less thought was the possibility of lateral relationships between learners (or indeed, between teachers). It is we think, primarily this kind of lateral relationship that the campus acts to support. For example, the kind of mutual peer surveillance that enables traditional exams to work is not dependent on any official flow of documents or communicative process, but rather on the simple lateral relationship of mutual recognition and non-recognition facilitated by the co-presence in the campus setting. We have also tried to use the notion of actor network, thinking to push this focus on lateral links beyond the notion of human interaction which is simply supported by the campus environment and to take seriously the role of the physical campus as an *actor* which does *work* (or various kinds – in the example we gave, this was primarily the work of symbolizing the university as an institution).

The literature on virtuality can easily be read as contrary to all things physical, such as the university campus. This is because the campus for some denotes a constraint on the reach of the university and a drain on its resources. The campus is, therefore, to this way of thinking, a limitation which needs to be transcended. Moreover, if we view education in terms of the creation, assembling, storing, transmission and processing of information (as does much of the literature on virtual universities), then the transcending of the campus is both possible and appropriate.

However, what we have found during our research, and tried to convey here, are the ways in which university-type education seems to resist such a treatment: it demands to be seen as other (or more) than information. Thus the university campus can equally well be seen as discreetly providing a wide range of educational resources. For instance, within conventional university life it would be difficult though not impossible to schedule a seminar before 9 am or on a weekend as this would have ramifications throughout the institution (opening buildings, turning on heating, providing catering, computer and lab support, never mind the question of whether colleagues and students would turn up – see Becker's (1982) discussion of a similar set of constraints in his book *Art Worlds*). Such temporal limitation might be contrasted unfavourably with the all-day, any-day timeframe of the Internet. Yet most of us live quite happily with, and indeed put to use, the constraints of traditional campuses. It is only when everyone has gone home and the university is closed, for example, that many of us find time to do research or writing. In this sense, the campus is best thought of not simply as a constraint but also, to borrow Brown and Duguid's felicitous phrase, as a 'resourceful constraint' (Brown and Duguid 2000: 246), one it would be premature to write off and which those developing distributed learning need to take seriously.

Note

1. Indeed, as we were first drafting this chapter, much of California, one of the richest and most technologically sophisticated places on earth, was being plagued with powercuts, the causes of which are complex but appear to involve various elements including the weather (cold winter and hot summer increasing demand for electricity), the price of oil (linked to the politics of Venezuela and the Middle East), the limitations of the state's regulatory regime, and so on.

5

The Online University as
Timely and Accurate Information

Introducing a new informational model of a university

It has become something of a commonplace to say that new information and communications technologies (ICTs) are transforming higher education. To date, much of this discussion has interpreted such change as something being added, as in the introduction of new actors, new forms of learning provision, new technologies and so on. However, while these technologies are, in an obvious sense, about the introduction of something new, they are also about the redefinition of many existing actors, activities and processes within universities. The example being used in the following extract is 'information':

> Currently most UK universities and colleges of higher education . . . are re-evaluating the way they gather, process and disseminate information for teaching, research and administration, for many this will mean radical change.
>
> (Allen and Wilson 1996: 239)

Information has always been assigned a crucial role within institutions; however, it constitutes one of the aspects that, through a process of redefinition, has come to take on an importance out of all proportion to its historical status (cf. Agre 2000a). There are, for instance, increasing pressures for institutions to think of themselves as 'modern organizations' (cf. Lockwood 1985; Barnett 2000). Figuring large in the emergence of this organizational view of universities is a demand for clearer roles, relationships and responsibilities, as well as more efficient work practices. Underpinning many of these changes are new forms of large-scale institutional computer systems and, of course, information. Indeed, a high-level report by the Joint Information Systems Committee (JISC), the body responsible for university computing in the UK, stated that information systems and, particularly, information have become the lifeblood of higher education institutions

(JISC 1995). As a resource on a par with labour, the JISC report commented, information should be considered as part of the infrastructure of universities. So central is information that JISC argues for the conflation of the role of information with the very 'vision' of the university.

In an attempt to analyse critically the information issue, this chapter reflects on an information system project being carried out at a university in the UK, which we refer to as Big-Civic. Narrowly defined, this project is concerned with the implementation of an enterprise resource planning (ERP) system, which is provided by a German software house, SAP, and is typical of those widely used by large corporations around the world. Recently, many universities in the UK and elsewhere have also turned to ERP as a means of replacing existing management and administration computer systems (Pollock and Cornford 2000).[1] We will call this system Enterprise. It includes a number of modules dealing with particular functions or aspects of the university, such as finance, human resources, project management and, eventually, student records. Enterprise is intended to replace a number of software technologies grouped around the university's existing Management and Administrative Computing (MAC) system. The project involves a wide range of actors, including the university's management and central administration, the software vendor itself and third-party consultants. At the heart of Enterprise is a large and complex relational database that will eventually contain and, importantly, 'integrate' information on the status of staff, students, buildings, equipment, documents, and financial transactions (cf. Davenport 1998).

Particularly relevant to this chapter is the way in which the Enterprise project team has come to conceptualize its task or mission, and to represent that mission both to itself and to the rest of the university. At one level, Enterprise is solely concerned with the provision of timely and accurate information throughout the university. While it might be argued that this aim is hardly surprising – the provision of information is, after all, the central purpose of information systems – at another level there are further, more interesting, even sublime, aspects to the Enterprise project. In point of fact, such is the nature of the mission being built around Enterprise that some have come to think of the system as a kind of virtual university.

It is seen as virtual for two reasons. First, within the system there is a large and complex model that has the form of a university, but without the thing itself. Instead of the heterogeneity of an organization full of competing goals and interests, in the Enterprise model every issue seemingly equates to an informational issue. For some within the project team, the informational model embodied within the system comes to represent the actual university. Second, at a more analytical level, the 'virtual' notion captures the idea of different models or worlds that coexist in a relation/tension, or the idea that one 'abstract' model can affect power through describing how that world ought to be (Carrier and Miller 1998). It is because of the introduction of the new model, in other words, that the old is seen as problematic. The interesting theoretical move, therefore, is in tracing the implementation of Enterprise as it begins to contribute to a shift from an old to a new model of the university. Indeed, it is through the very construction of Enterprise that a difference between the old and the new is achieved: the implementation of the system is simultaneously the construction of the new model and the destruction of the old.

Redefining the problem

The argument we put forward is that Enterprise is able to replace MAC successfully because various actors around the university have begun to accept the problematization as set out by the project director (particularly the notion that there is now within the university a new requirement for information). Importantly, we want to show how this is part and parcel of a larger discursive reorientation of the university as an 'information institution', where actors involved come to accept the inevitability of the model being offered (the informational model). To demonstrate the process by which everyone begins to speak – and think – in terms of information, we will be drawing on insights from the actor network approach introduced in Chapter 2.

According to actor network writers, to understand just how a technology becomes (or fails to become) a success we must follow and observe various innovators as they attempt to enrol others into their 'networks'. Such enrolments are typically based on one actor raising problems about the identity of another. Callon (1986a), for instance, discusses how environmentalists in the 1970s began to problematize assumptions held by a major car producer that consumers, increasingly motivated by environmental concerns, would still want to drive petrol-engine vehicles. They achieved this by outlining a scenario where new forms of battery-powered cars would be the only acceptable means of transport. In *Science in Action*, Latour (1987) characterizes successful innovation as what happens where one actor accepts and takes up the problem put forward by an innovator. In other words, the targeted actors have their goals and interests 'translated' to fit those of the emerging network. According to Callon then, the car producers shifted their interest from their current technology to those that were already being investigated by the environmentalists. For these writers, a technology, such as the battery-powered car, becomes a success when a sufficient network has been built for it, based on those who are willing to support it.

The utility of the actor network approach is twofold. First, it assists with 'redefinition', the process by which certain seemingly stable actors and entities are problematized and begin to take on new roles and identities. Second, it allows us to move beyond overarching general notions, such as technological determinism, to explain the way universities are changing. Rather, as is the purpose of this chapter, it helps to show some of the intricate ongoing work that makes it possible for one actor to convince others of the need for the university to change – and to modify its mode of working. Indeed, the mechanism by which one model of the university comes to dominate or replace another is related to the very practical work of loosening some associations (i.e. rendering ineffective or problematizing an existing network) and the simultaneous introduction and production of others. This shows how the construction of one new network is simultaneously the destruction of the old.

One of the key sources we draw on in the analysis is 'Information mythology', an article by the historian of technology Geoffrey Bowker (1994). In describing the early geology of some of the unexplored areas of Venezuela, he reveals the intricate socio-technical processes whereby scientists are able to turn local, unstructured knowledge about soil into 'global scientific information' which could be read, and understood, back in the laboratories of the Schlumberger Corporation. His argument is that the process whereby everything can be constructed according to the properties of information is not 'a preordained fact about the world' but 'it becomes a fact as and when we make it so'.[2] This is the very method by which certain actors come to accept the 'need for information' – or, indeed, the process by which a 'space for information' is constructed (cf. Porter 1994). In this chapter, we explore how such a process works in relation to the Enterprise system.

Reasons given for replacing the previous system

Big_Civic had been using a system developed through the University Funding Council's MAC initiative. This had been implemented in the early 1990s as a large-scale attempt to put in place, in a number of institutions, a computer system capable of handling both the 'needs' of universities and the production of standardized information that could be used to report to the UK government, which is the main funding body (Goddard and Gayward 1994). In 1995, the Big_Civic engaged the services of a well-known firm of management consultants to carry out a technical review of the state of the MAC system. This produced a document which, in common with the standard mode of consultancy reporting (cf. Bloomfield and Vurdubakis 1994), combines technical detail with a 'context'. For instance, before mentioning MAC's limitations, the preamble talks about the increases in student numbers, the advent of auditing, extreme competition for research funding, and so on. The document details how all of this is leading to demands for efficiency gains, and that the role of the computer system is no longer just presenting and accounting for the university to funding bodies. There is now a 'direct pressure' to spend more effort on 'management and administration', and to provide more data and information on 'relative performance'.

The importance of all this lies in the fact – and this is before reaching any of the technical detail concerning MAC's limitations – that the document can be read as an effort to signal that the university is working in a 'changing terrain', and that it should reconfigure itself – and its systems – in relation to this. The extent to which the notion of a changing terrain was accepted as sufficient reason to replace MAC with a new system is made evident in the following extract. Here we are listening to the project director during an away-day meeting providing the history of Enterprise to the project team:

> I'd like to say a few words about where we've come from ... [T]he World was changing, but I think the view [here] was – well, we hoped it would go away and it wouldn't change. Historically through the eighties, we under-invested in management information systems. Then MAC came along and it was seen as a panacea. It turned out not to be the magic bullet that many people had hoped, partly because the whole context in which MAC had been conceived was in the old model of higher education. The main funder was the government, and it was a 'command and control' system of reporting to government. Culturally and also, probably, technologically, it was an old model of the higher education system. And when we started moving into this new requirement for much more flexible information, MAC just didn't come up to scratch.

Interestingly, the project director is depicting a scenario in which there is an effortless shift from 'the World' and its external pressures, to the university, the model of the higher education system and, finally, to the MAC computer system itself – and a requirement for 'more flexible information'. To be precise, the picture he is painting is not one of a seamless shift, but a series of disjunctures. The university is out of step with the external situation (the rest of the world); the assumptions embodied within MAC are based on an old model of the higher education system – a model that is no longer appropriate for today's climate. All this has been highlighted since the university moved to this new need for flexible information. The response is apparently a straightforward one: bring all these factors into line through changing the system.

The mantra shaping the move from MAC to Enterprise

The management consultant's technical review document produced in 1995 was so wide-ranging in its criticisms of the MAC system that it was generally accepted by all as the definitive nail in MAC's coffin. The document's lengthy listing of MAC's technical and other limitations included such failings as: it appears 'old-fashioned;' it is slow; it lacks 'system bridges' between the centre and the faculties; and it does not compare well with commercial software with which people are already familiar. However, it was not until at least a year later that that the 'real' reason why MAC was to be replaced emerged. A senior member of the project team describes in a newsletter how

[Enterprise] software was chosen because it best suits our needs. It is flexible, easy-to-use and will provide *timely, accurate and accessible information* . . . MAC does not give us what we need to run efficient administrative and information systems . . . [j]ust one example is that it does not provide financial reports online to give people responsible for controlling budgets a real-time picture of their expenditure, instead they have to rely on paper reports, which are inevitably out of date. The difficulties this presents are well and widely understood. The advent of [financial devolution from the centre to departments] makes access to *accurate, timely information* even more important.

(emphasis added)

This was confirmed in the same newsletter by an end-user seconded into the project team:

My job is made more difficult by the fact that we have two systems in the department, each carrying account information that does not match . . . One of our big problems is not knowing our exact financial position. For example, there are always accounts which have been paid but have not yet shown up in the budget. Obviously this hinders planning . . . [the new system] will give us the opportunity to improve the way we manage our money and our people – and from what I have seen it looks very promising. For me, the biggest single advantage of [Enterprise] is its ability to provide *timely and accurate* financial *information* on research projects. I believe it offers significant improvements.

(emphasis added)

The recurring theme in these two accounts is that simply listing MAC's limitations is insufficient to explain why the system is to be replaced. It is seemingly not enough to say that the system 'does not provide financial reports online', or that it cannot 'give people responsible for controlling budgets a real-time picture of their expenditure'. Nor is it adequate just to say that while using MAC nobody knows his or her 'exact financial position', or that account information 'does not match'. One way of addressing this is to say that such limitations are not convincing enough; in terms of enrolling others, they offer little of what Latour (1988b) calls 'explanatory power'. In other words, in order to understand the outcome of all of this it is necessary to consider the relational context in and through which the story moves (cf. Woolgar and Cooper 1999).[3] Conceptually, this means that just what is to count as a sufficient explanation can only be understood as a result of 'usage': the way explanations of the reasons for change are accepted and taken up by others. So, just how do others use this story?

Whenever we are presented with MAC and its limitations, the story is always centred on the aims of the new project; these appear to manifest themselves in a single phrase that is repeated over and over again. The 'provision of timely and accurate information' mantra continually appears as the rationale, mission and justification for the project – in internal project documents, consultancy reports, communications from the team to the rest of the university and in team discussions. Ever present, at every meeting and in every document, this phrase has become, as it were, a member of the team, an actor.

What is more, the phrase is widely used within the team's strategy for communicating with the rest of the university, when discussing the move from MAC to Enterprise. Through its repeated usage, this phrase has come to stand for the reason for the replacement of MAC. For instance, to repeat the words from above: 'The advent of [financial devolution from the centre to departments] makes access to accurate, timely information even more important.' Similarly, 'the biggest single advantage of [Enterprise] is its ability to provide timely and accurate financial information on research projects.' The important question that needs to be asked here is: why were the aims of the Enterprise project taken up so straightforwardly?

How the project team used its mantra to drive Enterprise

There is little doubt within the project team regarding what Enterprise is about. In internal meetings, for instance, when discussions concern the goals of the project, or when questions come up about what it is they are trying to achieve, we invariably hear the repetition of the mantra. In one meeting, a senior administrator involved in the project was asked what she expected her department would gain from the implementation. She replied that Enterprise would provide her staff with 'information which is timely and accurate'. Another senior administrator articulated how such things as the 'production of the annual accounts and the [Higher Education Spending Authority] returns [should] hopefully become easier because [Enterprise] should facilitate better information and more timely.' This would help those out in faculties or departments who 'will get more timely information looking at their own accounts and plans against actuals'.

Enterprise is conceptualized according to a set of priorities that are 'known' and seemingly 'understood' by everyone within the team. Here, in contrast to the less convincing limitations attributed to MAC, the power of explanation of the mantra is strong. It holds in place the relationship between MAC and Enterprise as well as, arguably, the university, the model of higher education and their relationship to 'the World'. Indeed, such was the mode of use of this particular mantra that it was sometimes able to absent itself partially: the acceptance of the goals of the project were such that, at times, there was often little need to articulate the full vision, for instance by just stating that the project is concerned with the 'provision of all this timely and accurate etcetera, etcetera . . .'.[4] In actor network terms, this could be described as a successful translation because everyone is saying the same thing about the Enterprise system, and everyone has accepted the problematization of the MAC system, i.e. that it does not provide the right kind of information. This then begs the question of 'why' the informational mantra is able to work so well.

Our suggestion is that the phrase operates well because of the very 'resonance of information' within the university, in that it appeals equally to what Bowker (1994) terms the mundane and the mythical. In using these terms, Bowker is pointing to the way in which some information society theorists have attempted to redefine all human history as the history of information processing. This view redefines in terms of information processing the most prosaic bureaucratic processes, the nature of society and, in some cases, the very meaning of life (i.e. living systems as information processors). Analogously, we want to suggest that, there is a discussion within Big_Civic that characterizes Enterprise as both a simple information system and as the university itself. To exemplify what this means, we can return to the project director. Here, at the same away-day meeting, he is reading from a document containing a number of bullet points:

> I would like to spend a few minutes on the missions of the project...
> [The] first point: 'To provide consistent and timely information'. So this really is an information project. It is about information to run the business . . . Just going on to the various subheadings there so: 'Support the day to day'. The word day-to-day is an important word there. This is an information system which is also concerned with routine activities. There is still the basic 'running the business', which needs to be informed by, supported by, information systems.

Here, the project director is talking about the administrative processes you might associate with any large organization. He continued, emphasizing that information is concerned not only with the day-to-day running of the business:

> The second bunch of points is about the structure of the organization: 'bind together a decentralized organization'. Well this is the whole idea that the whole is more than the sum of its parts, that the University is not just a sheltered workshop where academics pursue their particular interests. It clearly has to be a supportive environment where people can do their own thing because if you really turn off those people then you are dead in the water. But, increasingly we're in a situation where we've both got to be entrepreneurial, but . . . good management is essential such that we do have processes which bind these entrepreneurial people into something which is the University of [Big_Civic]. And it's really a very important point where people have to have some sense of identity with the institution as a whole and some engagement, and agree to operate on the basis and principles that are there.

Here, we are witnessing the taking apart of one 'physical' model (the centralized administration) and the construction of another, seemingly virtual model. Once the project is implemented, many of the administrative activities currently carried out by the centre will be 'devolved' to departments; the centre is apparently not conducive to the entrepreneurial activity that is required. However, the worry is that once the administrative centre disappears, the university becomes nothing more than a 'sheltered workshop' for academics who are there only to pursue their own particular interests. Hence, the need for a 'supportive environment' – a 'something' – to 'bind these entrepreneurial people' into this entity called the university. But what is this something? Seemingly, it is informational processes. Academics are increasingly doing their 'own thing', the physical institution being for them nothing more than a constraint. Here, the university is (re)made according to the needs of these actors. Thus, we have a definition of Enterprise as both a mundane system that processes information and the basis for a new model (mythology?) of the university, a 'place' – or, rather, a set of processes – with which certain people can identify. The resonance of information is thus this causal link from the banal to the sublime (cf. Bowker 1994).

A second move leads from this. Not only is it a case of these 'entrepreneurial people' identifying with a university composed of informational processes: the actors themselves – and their relation to each other – are similarly constructed in terms of information. Indeed, according to the JISC report mentioned above, universities can be thought of as composed completely of 'information groups' (i.e. students, buildings, projects), 'information items' (i.e. teaching materials for a course) and 'information standards' (i.e. the attributes of groups and items).[5] What is more, these are also all 'performative' roles.

According to an internal document: 'Almost all organizational units, Faculties and Departments as well as central administration, will be collectors and generators, providers as well as customers of data and information.' This means that actors are conceptualized not in traditional terms (i.e. according to hierarchies) but according to their new 'delayered' duties towards information. This signifies that actors across the university (whatever their existing allegiances) can, in principle, align with everyone else according to the 'nature' of information. In other words (picking up on what was being suggested by the project director), these new informational roles are integrative: they act to 'bind together a decentralized organization'. What this is suggesting is that the hierarchy and nature of engagement of actors in this network are reconfigured; information has become the unifying principle in the university, the basis around which all actors are ordered.

The transition from an old to a new model of the university

Once established within the realm of the project team, the real work of implementing Enterprise began. This entails extending the mantra out into the university, which requires a stronger explanation to help the project team connect its mission with a straightforward outcome. The assumption is that the Enterprise system will enable the university, with all its problems, to move unproblematically towards the new model.

In terms of capturing how actors construct the existing model, the following conversation is illuminating. It is a conversation between the project director and the project manager (again taken from the away-day meeting). The project manager begins:

> Here people are very, very parochial, and if we are deciding whether we should be putting in an extra bit of a finance system as opposed to an extra bit of a student system, [the finance director] is going to vote for a finance thing and the student guys are going to vote for the student bit.

The project director follows up by agreeing, stating how he accepts 'absolutely the part about being parochial, I think that's the way it has been but in a way we've got to get away from this us and them model.' The project manager replies:

> The problem I found when I was on the [university's Information Technology] Committee was that you had a whole raft of people who had their own vested interests, and actually chaos was the one word I would hate to mention.

According to the project director, in place of this parochialism, vested interests and chaos, Enterprise will 'guide the internal decision making at all levels'. By this, he means that the university will 'move into a situation where people make decisions on the basis of information rather than prejudice, hunch, rumour [and] all those other things by which we currently run the business.' From an analytical point of view, the key point in all of this is the attempt to construct the university through the image of chaos. Information, it seems, will permeate 'all' aspects of the university, rendering decision making increasingly more visible and, therefore, subject to some form of internal benchmarking. This increased visibility is expected to displace, or translate, the chaotic and parochial university, the assumption being that through the increased provision of information some form of 'order' will rise from the chaos.

It is clear that all of this needs substantial unpacking.[6] Berg and Timmermans (1997) argue that disorder, for instance, does not precede order, but is constituted alongside order as a 'necessary and un-erasable parasite'. Their argument is one of the co-construction of problem and solution, meaning that the process is not the bringing forth of an established problem but the act of producing the problem with an eye to its eradication. In other words, through imposing the model onto the actual university, the order/disorder distinction is made possible. Within a university where information is seemingly freely and widely available, a 'whole raft of people' are readily seen as operating according to 'vested interests'. The model, by its very presence, makes the university appear disordered or, in other words, every order by necessity embodies its own disorder. It follows that to be wrong in this university (e.g. to be considered parochial, chaotic or self-serving) is to take decisions that are not based on information – that is, on information made visible according to the Enterprise system.

Living in the space and time of the virtual university

Reconfiguring the university

If we were to take at face value the notion that the introduction of information will begin to permeate every aspect of the work done, then a question that might arise would be: how might the new network space – where information is everything – begin to reconfigure this university? In order to benefit from all this timely and accurate information, certain forms of compliance would be demanded (cf. Wildavsky 1983). One example concerned with administration is the processing of paperwork. In a new way of working – which entails that information is always timely – forms cannot be left to pile up on desks until the end of the week or month, to be dealt with at a later convenient time; instead, all data must be entered when and where it is produced.

An example of what this means can be seen in the attempt to automate the student admissions system. According to the student system manager, the system 'will provide a workflow functionality so that we can get applications [for postgraduate study] in, we can scan them, we can send them around departments, selectors, selections teams, whatever. A decision can be put on which can be automatically coded.' Therefore, under the new system, applications 'should be acknowledged automatically and at the same time applicants should be advised of response times for the notification of decisions.' This is in contrast to the MAC system, where

> there is no clear process. Every department does things differently. There are long delays. There is the old argument 'do we lose post-graduate students because we don't turn decisions quickly enough and this kind of thing?' So you put a system in like this, [and] provided you could monitor and control it, is one of the benefits that you turn around decisions more quickly. Do we actually increase our recruitment?

The old model is seen as being without a clear process, and this leads to 'long delays'. If we were to turn around decisions in a real-time fashion, apparently we might actually increase recruitment. More conceptually, we are being presented with two images: the 'slow to react' student process versus a real-time system. What we are seeing is the creation of a difference between the processes carried out under MAC and those that will be in place with the new system: this is achieved by explaining the former according to what might be said to have caused it (delays, every department doing thing differently, etc.), and the latter in terms of what might be thought to result from it (quicker decision making, increased recruitment, etc.). This is interesting because it assumes that as a consequence of the introduction of Enterprise, the old approach to time will move straightforwardly towards the new real-time, and that each form of working practice is mutually exclusive. Further, it trades on the notion of Enterprise's diffusion into the university as akin to something like a 'blanket cover', when it would be more usefully thought of as one space, or network, coexisting with others.

We now expand on this as we think it offers some interesting insights into the relation of Enterprise to the rest of the university, or how one model is in tension with another.

How Enterprise extends itself throughout the university

In one important sense, Enterprise does begin to extend itself throughout the university when the users also begin to acknowledge that there is a need for a new system that produces more timely and accurate information. One might imagine that repetition of the mantra would be voiced with varying levels of commitment, enthusiasm or, perhaps, irony. Nevertheless, whenever we were present at meetings, the mantra was still repeated.[7] In other words, in perpetuating the mantra, the users begin to perform in this network. However, their commitment to the system is more ambivalent, as they do not perform the role that is expected of them. For example, the next quote is taken from a focus group, where a member of the support staff, having attended some of the initial training courses, is beginning to think how the system will work in her own department:

> Now when [Enterprise] comes in, the academics are going to have to conform to quite a lot of rules and regulations that they don't now. How on earth I am going to get my lot to do it, I do not know. Whether the centre has realized this, and is just not telling us what they are going to do about it, whether they are just going to trust to luck and hope that it works I just don't know. But, I am quite concerned about that. I mean it does create bad feeling if you are saying to somebody look you just can't just make an order over the phone, I won't pay for it if you do. It must come through the office, that's the system . . . And I can see that they are going to start screaming, as soon as I say to them, 'sorry, you can't do that any more you have got to do that now, that's what the system is supposed to do'.

What we have here is a powerful description of the way in which the Enterprise project is conceptualized as a mere mechanism for change, with the administrator portraying herself simply as a conduit for that change. The order embodied within Enterprise is expected to be reproduced throughout all departments – displacing existing modes of working with lots of new rules and regulations. While this type of account should not be disregarded, it seems that things were much more interesting than this in practice.[8] In one department, for example, it appeared that many of the new rules and regulations were themselves 'worked around' in order to slot into existing practices, rather than to reconfigure existing networks.

In the case of purchasing (i.e. stationery requirements, new equipment and travel tickets, etc.) the procedures had always been to obtain a new item or service through the production of a number of forms. In urgent cases, the practice would be flexibly adapted so that travel tickets, for instance, could be purchased first, with the appropriate forms raised later. This ad hoc practice is impossible under Enterprise, as all suppliers have received written instructions allowing them to supply goods and services only for those orders which are both printed on an appropriate form (the one generated by Enterprise) and bear a unique order number (again, generated by Enterprise).

In urgent cases, therefore, the administrator would generate the paper-work and a ticket, for instance, could be bought the same day. When the administrator is not available, however, the remaining support staff are faced with a problem. However, the administrator has circumvented this by designing, on her word processor, a copy of the Enterprise order form, which can be printed out at any time. This can be used when adorned not with the Enterprise order number, but with something she calls a 'pseudo number' or the 'secretarial requisition number' (a physical list of numbers kept by other members of the support staff). After this workaround has been carried out, the administrator is free to process the order through Enterprise in her own time.[9]

The significance of user workarounds

What do these workarounds tell us about what is going on?[10] At the very least, they teach us that the implementation would not be possible without such ad hoc modifications. At most, they indicate the nature of the new model and its relation to the old: that the real-time university where information is always 'up to date' is very much a performative notion. On the basis of what it knows and is told, the centre believes that the departments are working according to the real-time procedures; and as long as the users maintain these intricate workarounds, the university might as well be considered real-time. Thus, while the work of implementing Enterprise has involved both the production of a new model and the seeming destruction of the old, in many ways the established routines and practices (i.e. the old model) carry on as before. However, this is not to say that the university is the same as before.

To describe what this means we want to turn again to Bowker (1994), particularly his description of the building of a network of roads and pipelines through jungle terrain by the Schlumberger Company, as it searched for oil in Venezuela: 'The old state was often a mass of impenetrable jungle: the network rendered it, at key points, visible and accessible to the oil companies' (ibid.: 243). He goes on to describe how, within this network space, the companies were able to produce a 'local order' in the disordered space of the old state; this meant that no global picture was possible, as the scientists were only able to understand 'small pockets' of the jungle. Also, because the local order existed only in the places where the roads and pipes were physically located, this network would throw into stark contrast everything around it (i.e. from the point of view of the road, all the rest really was a jungle).

If we apply this to the Enterprise example, it might be said that the system, through the requirement that all decision-making activities be represented as information processes, is making the university, and the way that it works, visible and obvious to everyone. Further, because of the presence of the system, everything not already included within the system appears disordered – or much like a jungle (based on 'prejudice, hunch and rumour'). By establishing the informational model throughout the institution, it is therefore possible that all activities, practices, and processes not carried out according to the system will be found wanting in various ways.

Conclusion: is the university to be redefined as an 'information institution'?

While worldwide changes to higher education as a result of new ICTs are increasingly researched and reported, we still understand little of the particular dynamics associated with the implementation and use of mundane information systems – particularly the well-established, generic and corporate computer systems. Arguably, the use and adaptation of these systems have implications for the reshaping of institutional, organizational and individual identities. In particular, this chapter has attempted to show the means whereby a university can be redefined as an 'information institution'. In doing so, we also wanted to demonstrate that the process by which a large institution begins to think, talk and redefine itself according to the properties of information is not a fact about universities, but becomes a fact 'as and when we make it so' (Bowker 1994).

Empirically, we have focused on the replacement of one management information system with another, the reason for its replacement being that one does not provide the same type of accurate and timely information as the other. However, we argued that it is only through bringing together people disciplined enough to repeat an informational mantra that a difference between the two systems is achieved and a new information model is established throughout the university. While the complexity of the implementation allows for a certain amount of flexibility in how the users take up the various parts of the system (hence the discussion of workarounds as the continuation of the old model), now that the new model is established, all activity will be measured against this – and (of course) found to be wanting. Through the process of bringing everything together under the metaphor of information, Enterprise has therefore seemingly begun to allow the production of order in the chaos of the university.

Notes

1. While, as yet, there is little available systematic research on the spread of ERP systems to universities, anecdotal evidence suggests that many institutions across the globe have invested in, or are contemplating investing in, some similar form of industry-standard computer system. For example, SAP, the large German ERP supplier, is working with universities from Belgium, South Africa, Canada, the UK and the United States, to build the Campus Management system which can be integrated alongside other more established ERP modules (see Chapter 8).
2. His argument is that soil does not naturally translate in information terms but was constructed as such by scientists.
3. Woolgar and Cooper draw on Latour (1987: 29) here and his so-called first principle: 'the fate of what we say and make is in later users' hands'.
4. This was the project manager. After finishing his sentence with 'etcetera etcetera', there is a brief silence before he finally adds '. . . information to make business decisions at all levels.'
5. Within Enterprise, staff are conceptualized according to the supposed attributes of information as 'informational actors'. For instance, where we might have once thought about the university in terms of the vice chancellor, administration, academics, support staff, students, and so on, we are now encouraged to think in terms of the 'information manager', 'information custodian' or 'information user'.
6. A further example of what is being suggested here can be found in *The Control Revolution* by James Beniger (1986), who argued that the world is chaotic unless managers impose order on it through various technologies. Thanks to Phil Agre for bringing this work to my attention.
7. See the paper by Brown and Capdevila (1997) for a fascinating discussion of the repetition of the phrase 'the customer is king'. The only occasion when we were able to hear someone elaborate on the genesis of the phrase 'timely and accurate information' was during a conversation with a senior member of the project team. He suggested that the mantra originally started with the project director.
8. The previous quote is taken from someone just about to implement Enterprise in her department. We also conducted research in a department where the system was already being implemented.
9. This is a classic example of some of the 'interfacing work' carried out by individuals who span differing networks (cf. Gasser 1986).
10. For a detailed discussion of workarounds, see Pollock (1998).

6

Keeping Up Standards:
The Virtual University
is the University made Concrete

One danger is that we will standardize the wrong things.

(Agre 2000a: 199)

Introduction

The notion of a virtual or online university is a potent vision of the future of higher education. This university is seen as an institution that has torn itself free from the geographical confines of the campus, using the new communications technologies to connect learners, potential learners, teachers, researchers, alumni, employers, research funders and administrators in a flexible, ever changing network organization. This vision has captured the imaginations of academics, university managers, educational policy makers, corporate personnel, training managers and private entrepreneurs across the world. Steps towards the creation of the virtual universities have been taken in existing institutions, while a wide range of new institutions, many based on new networks of existing organizations, are being set up.

Before we rush to embrace the virtual university, and all the novelty that it brings, perhaps we should look too at the wider implications of virtuality in higher education, at what the move towards a virtual future means for higher education institutions, their structure and identity. As Agre (2000a) has pointed out, 'information and communications technologies create incentives to standardize the world'. What we want to do here is to build on this observation and argue that it is increasingly clear that the pursuit of the virtual university is having a major, perhaps paradoxical, impact on the institutional form and sense of identity of the university as it has developed in the twentieth century. Specifically, the application of the new technologies is generating a myriad of demands for reinstitutionalization of the university as a far more 'corporate', one might even say concrete, kind of organization.

The virtual and the university

What is the virtual university? One way of conceiving of a virtual university is as the decomposition of the existing university as a particular organization and place, and its recomposition as a set of wholly mediated relationships, underpinned by information and communications technologies (ICTs). Thus, it is the 'unbundling' of the various functions of higher education – for example, the recruitment and induction of students, the processes of teaching and learning, the assessment of those processes and the subsequent postgraduation support of the careers and alumni functions. These processes have traditionally been undertaken by the university as an end-to-end supplier.

Few believe that this totalizing vision of a 'university without walls' is currently achievable. Perhaps fewer believe that it is desirable. We are not without any number of critiques of this vision of the virtual university. Newman and Johnson, for example, identify this vision as being based on a 'naïve sociology' which 'ignores the role of apprenticeship and implicit craft knowledge in the generation of technical progress and scientific discovery' (Newman and Johnson 1999: 80), not to mention the role of face-to-face interaction and group socialization. Noble (1998) has likened the rush to embrace the virtual university to the discredited extension colleges of the 1930–50s, identifying this model as the 'digital diploma mill', a commodified travesty of public higher education driven by corporate greed and the self-interest of administrators (cf. Readings 1996). Winner (1998) pours ridicule on the whole process in his hilarious 'Automatic Professor Machine'.

For us, the notion of the virtual university is useful, not as a description of a particular type of institution, but rather as a description of a process or project which is being implemented, in different ways and with different intensity in existing universities, as well as in new institutions. Much of the excitement, exhilaration and fear (see, for example, Marchese 1998) concerns the establishment of new institutions – what we have called greenfield sites – with US for-profit institutions such as the University of Phoenix and the DeVry University as the exemplars. The bulk of the work of building ICTs into higher education, however, is taking place in established institutions – what, by contrast, we may regard as brownfield sites. In the jargon of industrial economists, it is 'in situ restructuring'. Cunningham *et al.* (1998), for example, found little interest among media and computing companies in establishing wholly new commercial higher education service provision, virtually all preferring to work *with* established universities (as suppliers or partners). The building of the virtual university is, then taking place predominantly within, and on the edge of, the well-established institutional context of established universities, albeit in close cooperation with technology vendors. From our point of view, it is also important to see this project as extending across the whole of the university: the virtual university is not just a matter of 'distance' or 'flexible' teaching and learning systems but extends into administration (finance, personnel, purchasing, estates, etc.), student recruitment and alumni management, research networks, library systems and so on.

The context of our research, then, has been the British university system. British universities are changing. They are having to react to a rapidly changing national and international environment (Schuller 1995; Newby 1999). Expansion in the 1990s has increased the number of students studying at higher education institutions (HEIs) by some 40 per cent in a decade. While student numbers have increased dramatically, increases in resources have been much more modest, leading to a declining per capita resource. The introduction of tuition fees for undergraduate students has made the financial relationship between the university and the student far more direct. Further, with university revenues tied to student numbers, students are increasingly being actively recruited rather than passively selected. Expansion has also changed the characteristics of the student body (Silver and Silver 1997): even undergraduate students are increasingly less likely to be conventional 18–21-year-olds engaged on a 'rite of passage'. Central government has sought, through the funding system, to provide encouragement for the recruitment of 'non-traditional' students, leading to a demand for different kinds of support and different procedures. Finally, students, both traditional and non-traditional, are seen as coming to universities with more demanding expectations, in terms of technologies and administrative efficiency.

At the same time that universities have sought to cope with expansion, and partly in reaction to the stresses that expansion has generated, there has been increasing demand from the state for accountability for public funds. The simple reporting of statistics by the central Higher Education Statistics Agency (HESA) has been augmented by an increasingly invasive set of audits. The Research Assessment Exercise (RAE) and the Quality Assessment Agency (QAA) have sought to systematically evaluate teaching and research, respectively, leading to the establishment of league tables. These audits directly (RAE) or indirectly (QAA) are determining to a larger and larger extent the real levels of resource in university departments. The growing professionalization of university teaching with the establishment of the Institute for Teaching and Learning (of which all teaching staff are being strongly encouraged to become members) also represents a response to the demands for accountability.

If there are increasing attempts to steer higher education by the British state, there are also pressures acting on HEIs from both above and below the national scale. At the international scale, universities are increasingly seeking to compete for lucrative foreign (non-EU) high-fee students (see, for one view of all this, Halliday 1999) and in an increasingly international labour market. In terms of international research contracts and grants, such as those from the European Commission, universities are in a much more competitive environment. Equally, at the local and regional scale, there is increasing recognition of, and state encouragement for, the role of

Figure 6.1   Models of universities as organizations

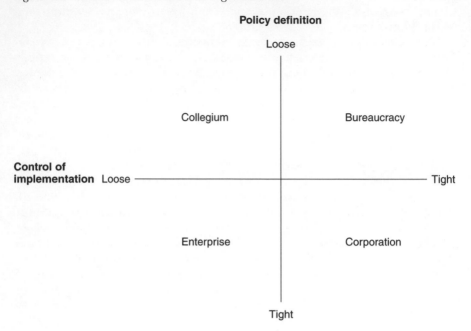

Policy definition

Loose

Collegium

Bureaucracy

Control of implementation Loose ———————————————————— Tight

Enterprise

Corporation

Tight

Source: McNay, 1995: 106

universities in the community, in technology transfer and in supporting local moves towards the transition to a 'knowledge-based' economy (see, for example, Goddard *et al.* 1994).

What does this mean for the university, for the way in which it is organized and for its sense of identity? The responses to these pressures have been widely analysed in terms of the growth of managerialism (Trow 1993), a transition that Parker and Jary (1995) have christened the 'McUniversity' (cf. Ritzer 1998), and which Shore and Wright (1999) characterize as a 'new and coercive form of authoritarian governmentality'. It is in this context that universities have sought to harness new technologies, a context in which the notion of the virtual university has suddenly become so very appealing.

Yet the picture is, in organizational terms, more complex than is suggested by a simple binary divide between the 'traditional university' and the 'managerial university'. McNay (1995) has provided a useful map (Figure 6.1) which, drawing on the management theorist Charles Handy, lays out what he calls 'the four cultures of the university', defined in terms of the degree of closure (tightness or looseness) in the their definition of policy and their control over implementation. McNay labels the four resulting archetypes as the collegium (loose definition of policy and loose control of implementation), the bureaucracy (loose policy definition but tight control over implementation), the corporation (tight policy definition and control over implementation) and the enterprise (tight policy definition and loose control over implementation).

While, as McNay notes, 'all four co-exist in most universities' (1995: 106), he sees a clear progression over the past decades in terms of the dominant culture, specifically from collegium to bureaucracy to corporation to enterprise, culminating in a 'fragmented' or 'atomized' institution characterized by small, task-focused work units, each having economic and managerial control over its own destiny, interconnected through 'benign computer and communication links' and bonding into larger organizations through 'strong cultural bonds' (ibid.: 114).

Our own research suggests that this image is too simple. In spite of more than a decade of managerialist reform, the collegium or the 'traditional university' remains an important self-image for university institutions, albeit one that is understood to be rapidly disappearing and which may never really have existed. Many of the university administrators and senior academics in managerial positions that we have spoken to describe their own institutions in terms that uncannily echo McNay's description of 'the classic collegial academy':

> A relative lack of co-ordination; a relative absence of regulations; little linkage between the concerns of senior staff as managers and those involved in the key processes of teaching and learning; a lack of congruence between structure and activity; differences in methods, aims and even missions among different departments; little lateral interdependence among departments; infrequent inspection; and the 'invisibility' of much that happens.
>
> (McNay 1995: 105)

Given this self-understanding, where is the university as an institution? Like Gertrude Stein's remark about Oakland, it often seems that 'there is no there, there'. There are, of course, elements of bureaucracy (rules, formal roles, etc.), the corporation (coordinated means–ends planning) and the enterprise (individual and collective entrepreneurship) present in all institutions. Nevertheless, the traditions of collegial self-management and the heritage of rule by committee mean that these tendencies are always to some extent held in check.

Under such conditions, then, it is clear that 'the university' must be seen as a highly heterogeneous institutional ensemble, which exists primarily in the heads of the people who constituted it, and in a myriad of locally negotiated practices and interactions. This traditional university, *as an institution*, often appears to exist only 'virtually'.

What we want to show in the next section is how, in the shift to the model of the virtual or online university, the applications of the new technologies, aligned with the pressures on funding and the imposition of increasingly short-term and instrumental policy goals by the principal funders of higher education, do not seem to be favouring the enterprise model. Rather, they appear to be reinforcing the establishment of a more 'corporate' form of organization where both policy formation and policy implementation are far tighter and goals, roles, identities, abstract rules and standard operating procedures are made explicit and formalized. It is in this sense, then, that we can say that the virtual university is a far more 'concrete' organization than its predecessor.

Building the virtual university in practice

What we have found as we have moved around a variety of universities examining ICT projects in teaching, research and administration, is that the pressures that are released by the use of computers and networks in the university generate demands for its reinstitutionalization in a more corporate form. The following three examples suffice to show how this is taking place.

Closing the triangle: Open University students and commensurability

The Open University (OU) is perhaps the nearest there is to a large 'virtual university' in the UK. Established in the late 1960s, the OU can claim to be the UK's largest university, with well over 100,000 students. On its own it represents 21 per cent of all part-time higher education students in the UK. OU students interact with the university in two main ways. Courses are developed by course teams, predominantly based at the university's Milton Keynes headquarters. This course material is then delivered using a mixture of media – books, television programmes, video cassettes, paper course packs, and, more recently, CD ROMs and material from the web – with the particular mix depending on the course. The second type of interaction with the university is through course tutors (increasingly known as assistant lecturers). Students and tutors have traditionally interacted through face-to-face meetings and over the telephone. Tutors are organized on a regional basis, some being permanent members of staff (staff tutors) but most being part-time (often lecturers in conventional universities and colleges). Many courses also have intensive summer schools.

While the OU has undertaken a lot of work centrally on the provision of course materials, it is only more recently that it has sought to use online technologies to mediate the relationships between tutors and students. Student–tutor interaction was, at the time we carried out our research, primarily facilitated by means of the First Class Conferencing system which gives students access to a number of 'online conferences' as well as by email. Assessment in the OU is generally in one of two forms: computer marked assignments (CMAs) and, more commonly, tutor marked assignments (TMAs). As the university has deployed the First Class system, and made increasing use of email, it has begun to adopt the practice of electronic tutor marked assignments (ETMAs) in which the student's assignment is submitted, marked and commented on electronically, before being sent to the university centrally and returned to the student by email.

This is, of course, a fairly mundane use of the new technology. Yet it, too, has had its effects, generating new demands on the university centrally. One OU staff tutor puts it as follows:

> As you know there are a lot of problems, a hell of a lot of problems . . . now because of the technology you get a greater flow of information. So you get thing like: a student gets 45 in Bristol, I got 75 in Newcastle. Then they start being able to compare. Now, this never happened before . . . With the advent of ETMA then a student has the script there marked in electronic form. So he can zap it off and they can compare comments. 'What my teacher said here, your teacher didn't pick that up' . . . You can try to standardize the marks, and we do that by giving pretty detailed marking schemes, . . . but for comments, and our teachers are judged as much on their commentary as on the allocation of marks . . . but the commenting is from minimal to reams – some tutors write loads and loads of stuff and they're still doing it in electronic form.
>
> (OU staff tutor – J)

What has changed here? The tutor's comments are simply encoded in electronic form rather than in ink. However, the effect of this recoding, coupled with the availability of email to the students, is to make those comments far more mobile. It is this mobility that renders them comparable by the student which generates demands for commensurate treatment. The effect on the university is to create a pressure to standardize not just the marking schema (which it has always done) but also the amount and format of the tutors' comments.

Indeed, as with the more traditional campus universities, staff within the OU are clear about the effects of the institution's increasing use of ICT to mediate between tutors, students, permanent staff and the administration. Another staff tutor describes the implications of ICTs for the OU thus:

> I think that they have found that if they suddenly say 'oh, everything's electronic' and just let everybody do their own things, you basically get chaos. And you cannot have chaos. The only way, then, is to have structures and models. What they are trying to home into is the kind of structures and models: what the course team, any course team, should be responsible for, what the remit and role of the tutor is and what the remit and role of the student is. That is formalizing things to a far greater extent.
>
> (OU staff tutor – I)

The key words of the corporate university are all there: structures, models, roles, remits, formalization.

That's a matter for policy . . .

The demand for a more corporate response from the institution is certainly not confined to the field of teaching and learning, but extends to new administrative and management systems.

A large redbrick single-campus university (Big_Civic, which we met in the previous chapter) is in the process of installing a new management information system. The Enterprise system, provided by the German software house SAP, has a number of modules, one for handling financial information, one for personnel information, one for research projects, one for student records, etc. The university is in the process of implementing the financial, human resource and research management modules, prior to adopting the student management module. For the pro-vice-chancellor in charge of the project, at least, the principal aim of the project is explicitly to 'bind together a decentralized organization'.

The implementation is being handled by an implementation team ('the team') made up of university staff and specialist consultants. Members of the team met with the 'faculty support team' and representatives of the departments that were going to pilot the new system. The consultants had a set of 'workflow process diagrams' which describe the proposed sequences of events by which tasks such as setting up a research account, raising a purchase order or issuing an invoice would take place within the new system. Each step of the process was described in detailed flow diagrams, indicating which parts of the process would take place 'on the system' and which take place 'off the system' as well as constraints on who can undertake which tasks. Each of the workflow process diagrams is discussed with the departmental representatives and faculty team. The aim of the session was to clarify the workflow processes, iron out any problems which arise, and identify who does what.

As the meeting moves through the workflow diagrams, a number of basic rules of the system are made clear (for example, two separate logins are required to complete each and every transaction – the same login cannot order and receive goods). At some points the workflow diagrams are amended to better reflect the current practice (although this amendment tends to happen more often with 'off system' events). At a number of points in the process it became clear that there was more than one way, in current practice, in which a particular step in the process was being handled. If the issue could not be resolved one way or another, the consultant leading the meeting identified the issue as 'a matter for policy' – a matter on which a definitive ruling must be given by the university centrally.

What seems to be happening here, as the computer system is rolled out through the university, is more than a mere standardization of working practices and clarification of roles. Rather, the rollout of the system generates a constant flow of demands for 'policy'. Indeed, each of these requests for a central university policy decision was logged centrally by the team in a database and passed on to the university management to resolve. The process therefore not only sees the 'tightening up' of roles and procedures (implementation), but also demands a tightening up of *policy* which will apply, not locally, but across the university, in effect calling the university into being as a far more corporate institution. We might almost say that the rollout of the system is requiring the simultaneous rollout of a new (and more standardized) institution to host it.

(Re-)creating the institution

These pressures for a more standardized and corporate kind of university are happening not just as a result of the cumulative (and perhaps unforeseen) consequences of the move to a more computer-mediated institution. In some institutions, as the next case makes clear, they are quite consciously planned as such.

City_Campus, formerly a polytechnic, has established a programme on excellence in the use of ICTs. This programme, called Excellence in Use of C&IT, has a number of strands concerned with infrastructures (the Internet as a 'global campus'), the commercialization of knowledge, support services (a multimedia authoring laboratory) and a set of experimental flexible learning projects. While there were a number of sites of experimentation with new technologies in the university prior to the start of the programme, the programme was founded to link up, support and extend this experimentation across the whole organization. The programme's director describes it thus:

> Excellence in Use of C&IT . . . was a way of going right across faculty and departmental boundaries, breaking them down. And that's the whole ethos behind the project – that we want to share experience across the University rather than reinventing wheels in every little corner.
>
> (Programme director)

A major component of the programme is a number of experiments in using new ICTs for 'flexible and distance learning'. The main concern for the programme managers, however, is not to have a raft of successful projects, but rather to develop models of distance and flexible learning that can be 'scaled' up to the institution as a whole. A major sponsor of the programme describes it thus:

> What we wanted out of it was not some projects that in their own terms were successful and maybe glamorous in the world outside, but models that might be scaleable for the institution for distance and flexible learning, that could survive the transition from the enthusiasts – who will make it work come what may – to regular line provision.
>
> (Service director)

The ultimate aim is thus to establish the precise structures, roles and responsibilities necessary to implement online learning. The programme director describes the aims of the project as follows:

Currently, because of the way the programme is going – and it is
a development programme and I think that we'll stress that – a lot
of the pseudo-admin work has been done by academic staff. They're
doing the tracking, they're setting the things up. But to me, when
you run it, as probably they will run it in the future, it would be too
expensive for them to do that so the administrators would need access
rights and they could do some of the humdrum day-to-day checking
of whether work's come in, how many times a student has logged on
etc. etc. So we will need to define, and I think rewrite, the roles and
responsibilities.

(Programme director)

The familiar issues of commensurability and consistency arise. As the director
of City_Campus's Information Services Department (a joint library and computer services unit) puts it: 'We ought to be able to tell a student in Kuala
Lumpur, "if you become a student of [City_Campus], what's the deal" and
that ought to be consistent across the piece'.

Once again, the key words, in this case much more explicitly coded into
university policy, are to rebuild the institution around the technology. The
director of information services is again clear about all of this:

The thing that trips it up isn't that the technology doesn't work, its
trying to recreate the organization so that it can usefully apply the
technology, rather than crippling [the technology] so that we can do
things the way we did before.

(Service director)

The goal then, is to make the whole organization 'very corporate by university standards'. On probing for the service director's understanding of the
notion 'corporate', we elicited the following reply:

rather than making a whole lot of decisions in various places and after
the event hoping that they fit together, rather you coordinate . . . [A]ll
those decisions are made more collaboratively in the context of the
whole. That's what I understand by it.

(Service director)

What the programme seeks to achieve, then, is coherence at the centre,
decisions made 'in the context of the whole', 'consistent across the piece'.

Conclusion: the virtual university is the university made concrete

What does all this mean for the university as an institution? Building the
virtual university appears to require, at least in the first instance, the construction of a far more corporate structure capable of coordinated action
with formalized roles and standardized practices. Indeed, our research

suggests, this does seem to be the case: as we argued in Chapter 3, attempts to build the virtual university from the bottom up, course-by-course, without reconstructing the basic structures of the university, appear to be very slow, labour-intensive and highly prone to failure. Yet perhaps this should be no surprise. The very notion of information, which sits at the root of the notion of a virtual university (see Chapter 5) and its ability to abstract from place the specific, the parochial – (see Chapter 4) contains within it a powerful incentive to formalize, to standardize, to make explicit, to make concrete. Returning to Porter's vision of a 'world of information' as a 'world of standardized objects and neutralized subjects', contrasted with 'local sites where skill and intimate familiarity with people and things provide the most promising route to success' (Porter 1994: 221), we are prompted to ask to what extent is this pacified world, and the concrete structures necessary to create it, compatible with the wider processes of higher education?

7

Customizing Industry Standard Systems for Universities

Nothing is, by itself, either reducible or irreducible to anything else. There is no equivalence without the work of making equivalent.

(Latour 1988a)

Introduction

It is a truism that universities form one of the oldest established institutions in the western world – far older, for example, than the joint stock company or indeed the bureaucracy of the nation state – and despite changes in form, function and fashion, the very latest universities retain some links, however tenuous, with their medieval forebears. Equally, while bodies bearing the title 'university' vary dramatically in terms of their structure, function and form, the fact that they choose to label themselves as universities rather than as any one of a number of alternatives, suggests a desire to capture and share in that thousand-year-old tradition.

On the one hand, then, it is tempting to see the university as something different or set apart from other organizations – as a unique institution in the modern world. Balderston, for instance, describes how, historically, universities grew as a type of institution that was, and still is to some extent, 'distinctive' with an 'autonomous place in society and the right to choose its members, settle its aims, and operate in its own way' (1995: 2). On the other hand, it is also clear that there are many similarities between universities and other organizations. As Lockwood has put it: 'universities as organisations face many problems common to most modern organisations' (1985: 29), including, for instance, the problems of coordinating resources, controlling costs, of stimulating and facilitating enterprise among staff, and so on. Thus, it might be argued, that since universities have problems common to a wide range of organizations, then the standard tools of contemporary organizational analysis and institutional management – including computer systems used by large corporations around the world, such as enterprise resource planning (ERP) systems – can be applied similarly in universities.

Some have attempted to resolve this issue of differences and similarities in an interesting way. Lockwood, for instance, argues that universities are unique only to the extent they possess a certain *combination* of common characteristics which he lists as complexity of purpose, limited measurability of outputs, both autonomy from and dependency on wider society, diffuse structures of authority and internal fragmentation (1985: 31–2). Whereas organizations in general might possess one or more of these characteristics or components, it is the particular combination of the components within universities that makes universities 'unique'.

The aim of this chapter is not to attempt to resolve this issue of similarity/difference in one way or another (as if that were at all possible), or, indeed, to evaluate the appropriateness of new forms of computer systems for universities. Rather, through reporting on a fine-grained study of the implementation of an ERP system within a university, we want to explore how some of these differences and similarities are actively constructed and 'brought into being'. Initially conceived according to a narrow set of assumptions about how organizations operate, ERP systems have, as they have been continually applied to new contexts, expanded to include an ever increasing range of organizational characteristics and functions. These characteristics are embodied in the system as modules and ready-made business process templates and, as is made clear in supplier brochures, are seen as being applicable to a wide variety of user organizations. In some senses, this might be thought of as the practical implementation of Lockwood's view: such systems are fundamentally based on the notion that organizations contain common elements and through combining the various modules or templates an organization can create for itself its own 'unique solution', yet still have a fully supported computer system in which each individual component is 'best of breed'. As we will see, this is not, or at least not for universities, the case.

In the institution where we carried out research for this chapter, many of the university's policies and processes underwent a process of standardization. This, we want to argue, could be seen as a course of action where procedures, processes and discourse are rendered similar to those embodied in the system and, consequently, other forms of organization.[1] Although, as we want to demonstrate, this occurs in part through conscious choice, it also happens by 'default'. Reducing institutional diversity is invariably complex. Two further aims, therefore, are to demonstrate the particular ways in which the university has engaged with the system, and to show how the ERP system is also subject to much change. Both these processes are accompanied by a struggle, where this construction of difference and similarity occurs not simply within the close confines of the project team (although this is an important part of it) but as the outcome of a complex set of relationships the university has with the system and its supplier, its various departments and other institutions involved in similar implementations. Our argument is that managing this process has become a key task, and difficulty, for universities.

Before presenting our empirical material, however, it will be useful to provide, first, a brief review of the theoretical notions and concepts that have informed this study, second, background information on the institution and the project under way, and finally, a brief description of ERP systems.

Theoretical background: studying 'translation' and 'biographies'

The chapter focuses on the relationships developing between system suppliers, whose aim is to extend their technologies into as many different settings as possible, and higher education institutions, which are intent on capitalizing on the benefits of standardized software while maintaining, supporting and, in many cases, updating specific institutional and organizational features. In order to capture the various dynamics operating here – the introduction of new roles and work practices, as well as the reshaping of various identities – we have adopted a fine-grained, micro-sociological approach that is informed by a range of perspectives from actor network theory, the sociology of science and technology, and studies of material culture.

As yet, few studies of the implications of such large-scale systems for universities have been carried out. Cunningham *et al.* (1998) mention the potential of ERP for reshaping organizational aspects, but do not present empirical evidence to illustrate or substantiate such claims. Heiskanen *et al.* (2000), by contrast, have conducted a detailed study but conclude that such industry standard systems are inappropriate as universities as organizations are 'unique, particularly in terms of their decision making processes' (2000: 7). However, as we want to argue, the significance of these systems would be better appreciated and understood if we were to resist viewing universities (or, for that matter, computer systems) as stable entities or as having characteristics that are 'given in the order of things' (in the manner of Lockwood or Heiskanen *et al.*). Instead, we want to explore some of the processes that might generate these characteristics as 'effects'. Theoretically, this move has most famously been explicated in the work of Norbert Elias, Michel Foucault and, more recently, in actor network thinking, where it has been painstakingly shown how the development of scientific, organizational and bureaucratic *processes and practices*, simultaneously involved the development of scientific institutions (Latour 1988a), organizations (Cooper and Law 1995), and the 'modern state' (Bowker and Star 1999).

Moreover, a number of terms and concepts are synonymous with the actor network approach, including viewing the world in terms of the emergence of competing 'actor networks', where various elements are brought together or 'enrolled' into an assemblage, which is capable of 'acting as one' (Latour 1987). As part of this network building, there are continuous processes of multilateral change or 'translation', where one actor will attempt to channel the goals of others in new directions. In doing so, however, an actor will often find his or her own route redirected. Finally, the approach has also fruitfully suggested that it is not only human beings, but also 'things' that can undertake the required work of 'translation' of interest necessary to build and sustain actor networks, and thus that non-humans should also attain the status of actors (Callon 1986a).

As well as drawing on the notion of actor networks, we also want to capture something of the history or 'biography' of these systems – both what they bring with them and what this means for the new sets of users. Appadurai (1992), and particularly Kopytoff (1992), writing from the perspective of material culture studies, use the notion of biography to describe established artefacts as they move around and are adapted and redefined according to the needs of each new place. Biographies, they argue, highlight the various relationships and meanings an object established among one community may have for actors and communities in different places. As Kopytoff emphasizes: 'what is significant about the adoption of alien objects – as of alien ideas – is not the fact that they are adopted, but the way they are culturally redefined and put to use' (1992: 67). The biography of a car in Africa, to use the example given in Kopytoff's paper, reveals enormous amounts of information about 'the relationship of the seller to the buyer, the uses to which the car is regularly put, the identity of its most frequent passengers and those who borrow it', and so on. Crucially, all these details would 'reveal an entirely different biography from that of a middle class American or Navajo, or French peasant car' (1992: 67).

The benefits of a biographical approach to objects, combined with the actor network perspective, is that it 'sensitizes' us to the various dynamics in play as these systems are translated from a general or commercial organizational context to a specific, university setting. This is in keeping with the approach suggested by Williams (1997), who argues against those studies that emphasize simply the 'flexibility' of technology, as well as its potential for readaptation to a new setting, without considering the complexities and dynamics of what he describes as a technology's broader social and historical context [2]

Restructuring the university, customizing an ERP system

The acquisition of well-established, generic and corporate computer systems is increasingly common – and not just among universities. After more than 30 years of computer systems development, in an ever growing variety of institutional and organizational settings, few systems are developed from scratch. Rather, most large-scale institutional computer systems are constructed by adapting existing elements to new organizational contexts. Firms and organizations no longer commission and build bespoke systems and packages, instead adapting general solutions to their local context (cf. Brady *et al.* 1992). Having access to 'tried and tested' software, as well as the benefits of constant upgrades and new products, is seen to outweigh the lack of specificity associated with such systems. ERP systems are a case in point: initially conceived for use within manufacturing firms, their diffusion among other organizations has been rapid, such that they are now seen as the *de facto* standard for the replacement of legacy systems in multinational companies (Parr and Shanks 2000).

The institution on which this chapter is based is a large civic university based in the UK, which we call Big_Civic. The rationale for embarking upon the project, as given by the pro-vice-chancellor in charge of the project, was both to replace existing systems that were seen as limited and to support a fundamental restructuring of the institution's information management system as recommended in a consultancy study. Related to this, it was also hoped that the new system (called Enterprise) would encourage the development of procedures and practices more commonly found in large corporations, so-called best business practice:

> I think the reason why all the bigger universities are beginning to go towards [Enterprise], is that it has come out of a multinational environment where in essence what [multinational companies] are involved in doing is having highly decentralized structures where you're giving your line managers a lot of autonomy and responsibility within a framework of an overall corporate entity; where the role of higher level managers is to have an oversight of the business as a whole and take strategic decisions and so on.
>
> (Interview with pro-vice-chancellor)

The Enterprise system is produced by a large European software house and includes a number of modules dealing with particular functions or aspects of the university, including finance, human resources, project management and (eventually) student records. The project involves a wide range of actors, including the university's management and central administration, the software vendor itself, and a number of third-party consultancy companies. At the heart of Enterprise is a large and complex relational database that will eventually contain information on the status of staff, students, buildings, equipment, documents and financial transactions.

Customization

Proponents of ERP systems have argued that, in terms of organizational fit, such systems have universal applicability (cf. Lozinsky 1998). However, despite such extravagant claims, there is a growing body of evidence to the contrary. Adopters often find that the assumptions embodied by these systems about the nature of organizations and the ways in which they operate, run counter to existing structures and work practices.[3] The suppliers of these systems will, in truth, often acknowledge and try to accommodate organizational variety through the continued addition of new and sector-specific modules. Moreover, many of the more local incompatibilities between the system and the organization, from the vendor's point of view, can be reconciled through customization. Indeed, these systems are marketed on the flexibility of their modular design, as well as the ability to choose from hundreds of 'business process templates', and the tailorability of the various parameters and settings. A supplier brochure describes this in more detail:

> From a broad spectrum of functions and alternative business processes, you select the modules that you want to mould into an internally consistent organizational system for your company, depending on your specific requirements . . . We match its core processes to your needs by customizing additional applications, which we or our partners implement for you. Or your own IS [information systems] staff can do the work simply and easily with the [Supplier Specific] Development Workbench, which is an integral part of the [Enterprise] system.

A user organization is thus supposed to be able to choose from the 800-plus ready-made business processes, some of which have already been tailored to match certain sectors,[4] and then to customize locally the resulting assemblage.

Unsurprisingly, the reality of customizing these systems is somewhat different. Pollock (forthcoming), for instance, notes some of the problems that arise when there are ambiguities regarding which parts of a system can be modified, or there are 'blurred' boundaries about the roles of designers and implementers (cf. Trigg and Bodker 1994). Moreover, just as modifying the 'wrong' parts of a system can lead to problems, so too can customizing industry standard systems 'too much' (cf. Tierney and Williams 1991; Brady *et al.* 1992, Hanseth and Braa 1998). Heavy customization can mean that a system is taken away from supplier standards, meaning it will be difficult to make use of later upgrades or new system functionality, the very reason why many systems are acquired in the first place.

Unregulated and excessive local customization is at one end of the scale. At the other end lies the problem of systems not being tailored at all. There is, for example, growing evidence to suggest that because of the sheer number of organizational and technological discrepancies that arise during attempts to customize (cf. Hanseth and Braa 1998; Ciborra 2000; Walsham 2001), and the complexity and time-consuming nature of each modification, most adopters simply end up fitting their organization to the system rather than the other way around (Koch 1999; Markus *et al.* 2000). One study, for instance, found just 5 per cent of organizations, out of 1,000 questioned, had attempted major customization (Davis 1998). It seems that rather than attempt to reconfigure each and every aspect of a standardized system (the various templates, system parameters, authorization profiles and so on), implementation teams simply accept those 'default' features embodied within the system – an example of what one author has called the 'power of default' (Koch 1999).

In what follows, we turn to Big_Civic's engagement with Enterprise. First, we consider how the university (its hierarchy, senior management team and various committees) attempted to take customization decisions. Then we analyse a new student management module called Campus Management that the supplier is in the process of building in conjunction with Big_Civic and other pilot universities.

Building the system and the university

When the chips are down and you've got to deliver, the collegiate model doesn't work.

(Enterprise project director)

When we conducted the early parts of our research, Big_Civic was in the process of implementing the financial, human resource and project management modules prior to adopting the student management module. The work of adapting and expanding the existing software to the new context of the university involved both non-technical and technical staff from the university, programmers from the supplier of the system and third-party consultancies. In this adaptation work, information about existing management and administration processes would be collected and passed down the chain to the programmers, who would pass back code based on their understanding of the information they had received. In practice, however, this often proved to be a considerable hurdle. The problem was that, in some senses, for the suppliers *there was no university there to fit to the system.* What we mean by this is that, in contrast to the highly defined processes, hierarchies and roles embodied in the system, the university is made up of locally negotiated practices and interactions, many of which are difficult to capture accurately or to articulate in the language of ERP (see for example, McNay's (1995) description of the traditional collegial campus in Chapter 6).

This point is well exemplified by the implementation team's attempts to uncover the recent history of university practices regarding the handling of student fees so that they might be examined, rationalized and reformatted for inclusion in the system. In one conversation, for instance, the team is trying to work out the process for setting and administering fee categories, where categories had been established on the existing system but where it was not obvious why they were there, who had made decisions, or even where the data had come from. As one working document recorded it:

> Every degree programme is currently assigned to a fee category within MAC [the existing system]. However, the process by which new programmes are allocated to categories is unclear and haphazard. The fee category is an important parameter in the proposed system.

Further investigations provided no clues, and thus the team came to the conclusion that the staff responsible for inputting the data were simply 'making them up'.

The entire process of allocating, approving, checking and raising fees is not sufficiently clear. No one individual/group has a complete overview of the overall process and purpose.

Thus, instead of simply taking existing practices and including them in the system, the management team had to formulate a policy for student fees and implement this across the entire institution. In the previous chapter we described how there were many such 'demands for policy' generated by the system. So many, in fact, that they had to be stored centrally on a database to be dealt with at a later date. What appeared to be happening here, as the computer system was rolled out, was a standardization of working practices and roles. In other words, the suggestion is that the process of customizing Enterprise involves both the building of a university-specific system and the rebuilding of the university: the rollout of Enterprise is requiring the simultaneous rollout of a new (and more standardized) institution to host it.

This 'co-production' of system and university is a complex process, however. As we found out in a later phase, these demands for policy were so copious that many of the requests simply remained on the database without senior management ever having the time to deal with them. The committee overseeing the system rollout (made up of a number of pro-vice-chancellors, the registrar, bursar, various deans and senior administrators) did meet once a week intending to resolve these demands but, in the words of a project administrator, 'the Committee were getting 20 issues a week to resolve and therefore they usually did not get past the first or second one on the agenda'.[5] In other words, as the rollout of the system begins to highlight the variety of local practices around departments and these cannot be reconciled within the system, the sheer number of issues generated provides a problem for those attempting to decide on the future direction of the university. As a result, most of the issues have to be resolved within the project team on more technical grounds, meaning that the team had to deploy its own criteria while configuring the system. And, in many cases, this meant just accepting default settings.[6]

Here, then, is a further elaboration of the power of default view of implementation: because the university cannot decide on the details of the system, the decision is defaulted to the project team and, then, ultimately onto the system itself. In terms of the construction of uniqueness of universities in relation to organizations more generally, the university, through its relationship with the system, emerges almost by default as an organization to be treated like any other.

Where do defaults come from?

So far we have looked at how the system is implemented according to the power of default, but as yet we have not discussed where these defaults come from. Enterprise systems, to recap, are based on the practices and processes of many different organizations, and, because of this, they are often described as embodying 'best business practice'. One element that is not available within Enterprise, however, is templates for one of the core functions of universities: the management and administration of students. In recognition of this 'discrepancy', the supplier is currently developing new functionality that can be integrated into Enterprise, a student management module called Campus Management.

What is interesting about the design of the student module is that it is conceived around the idea that students are to move from being passive objects of administration to becoming one of the main groups of 'active users' (Pollock and Cornford 2000). This raises the following question: if students are to be one of the system's primary groups of users, then how did its designers understand their role and identity, as well as their relationship to the university and its staff? Moreover, in conceptualizing the student as a user, were they to assume that students had the same competences, needs and interests as, say, an employee working within a commercial organization, the typical user of the Enterprise system? How, in other words, did they manage this difference between the typical users of the Enterprise system and the student as a unique type of user? Indeed, was there a difference?[7]

As part of the process of learning about students, a requirements analysis phase was conducted. This entailed a series of visits to pilot universities where key actors were interviewed and observed while carrying out their work. In addition to this, hundreds of questionnaires were dispatched, asking more specific questions about system access for those students based on campus, what information was relevant to them, what they could and could not see, and so on. In other words, in developing this new functionality there was a recognition that universities were not, after all, like other organizations. And, in this sense, it is not accurate simply to say that universities face problems common to other organizations. Clearly, within the Enterprise system there was no element to deal with the specific issue of students.

No default, however, is completely remade anew. Even though the supplier was in the process of designing and writing software for the new student module, 'new' is meant in a loose sense here. The module was in fact a reworked version of the Training and Events Management module, a system used to run internal training programmes within commercial organizations, and the Real Estate module. As such, Big_Civic found many aspects of the software incompatible with pre-existing institutional structures, processes and the characteristics and identities of actors. Most directly, Enterprise is structured around business notions such as supplier, employee and customer, and while these may share some of the characteristics of categories found in universities they do not map straightforwardly. In one part of the system adapted for the management of accommodation on campus, for instance, the student was in effect conceived of as a special type of employee, one who was undertaking a long-term training course and thus permanently renting a room.

> Until now the Real Estate module has always been referred to for student housing. This only contains the functionality to 'let' rooms (very commercial). For some universities this is not enough. Student rooms are often part of student aid. A lot of extra activities have to be organized in association with this (e.g. meals).

University staff rejected this conceptualization, pointing out that it did not capture the complexity of the student–university relationship. At some pilots, for instance, students do not 'rent' rooms but receive accommodation as part of wider aid packages. Similar sentiments were expressed at Big_Civic:

> [T]he Real Estate Module is so far removed from our requirements that SAP [the supplier] would do better to start again from scratch than try to adjust the existing module. The most obvious shortcomings of Real Estate for us are: The module is designed for the commercial sector where long term lets of 12 months or more are standard. It is not designed for the levels of volume and turnover that characterise the student market and, even more obviously, the conference market. In short, Real Estate does not set out to be a retail booking system, which is what we are looking for.
>
> (Internal memo)

Examples such as this led to tensions among prospective users, some of whom described the system as simplistic and overly commercial. More generally, it appeared that the supplier just did not know enough about universities, their particular characteristics, and the nature and role of actors within them to be able to translate the module successfully. The system supplier admitted as much by announcing how it had 'severely underestimated the complexity of the higher education sector'.

Students appear to be something of a 'residual' category for the system (cf. Bowker and Star 1999). On the one hand, there is an explicit recognition that universities are different: they have components not found in other organizations (students). On the other hand, there is also a feeling that, at a basic level, there are lots of similarities, that students are, or should be, or could be made to be, very much like the more familiar (to the supplier) category of employee. More generally, we might say that despite this recognition that students (and thus universities) *are* different, they are, nevertheless, always being rolled back towards a default, i.e. the history of Enterprise appears to win through.

Coping with the specificity of universities

There is one more aspect that we wish to expand on. The supplier regularly tested the system with the pilots and early adopters. For this testing, university personnel would periodically travel to an arranged venue where they would sit in a large classroom and work through test versions of the system. We observed one such meeting. In fact, unbeknown to the pilots (and us), this was to be the last workshop of this kind. Most of the session was devoted to demonstrations of new software, with consultants asking for comments on whether this or that aspect of the system was appropriate to each institution. A second aim was to find some form of consensus about what common needs there were, if any, among universities.

Finding a concept

One method of doing this was to develop a concept. For example, there was a discussion around the issue of 'holding', the process whereby a student may not be permitted to re-register for a new academic term because of outstanding library or tuition fees, a failed exam or unpaid rent, etc. The issue was the extent to which holds should be input manually or be triggered automatically by Enterprise. According to one consultant, manual inputs are a 'system limitation', therefore, if universities could only 'better define' their specific holding processes, then, the procedures could be 'automated'. She begins by asking for comments on what currently happens in various situations:

> *Consultant*: Students with bad marks. What do you do with them, leave them in limbo, or give them a second chance?
> *New Town University*: Depends on timing. If just before a session and there is no chance of them bettering their mark, then we refuse them. Or, alternatively, we could say we've not decided yet. That is not a hold but a 'waiting status'.
> *City University*: If you are doing something that might pick up your grades?
> *Consultant*: I wouldn't call that a hold, that's a 'provisional situation'.
> *Rural University*: We have a 'partial hold', so holds affect some things . . .
> *Large Campus University*: Isn't that a 'half-hold' . . .

From the discussion, it is evident that the pilot universities each have a diverse set of rules and practices regarding how they currently process holds. After some time discussing each of the variations, the group appeared to be in a state of confusion where the participants are no longer sure exactly what a hold might be – is it a 'waiting status', a 'provisional situation' or 'a half-hold'.[8]

Interestingly, and perhaps rather counterintuitively, it is the supplier, and not the universities, who attempts to promote this diversity. Indeed, the participants were becoming increasingly frustrated by the supplier's attempts to understand each and every difference among all the universities present. For the supplier, such a process is useful as it allows the concept (i.e. the default) to become more robust and, thus, applicable to the widest variety of higher education institutions. For the pilots, the process, while drawn out, appeared to be similarly useful as it ensured that all of those present would be able to find their own unique solution within the standard module.

In a later stage, however, a process of closure begins to set in around the extent to which each pilot could continue to shape the module. In contrast to the search for robust concepts, each new request began to be labelled 'university specific'. Low Country University, for instance, reports to the other pilots how:

> We have the feeling that it's becoming a strategy to try to label issues as 'university specific until proven differently'. Should it not be the other way around? Should [the supplier] not search for generic concepts behind the specific situations at the different pilot universities?

Moreover, since there were to be no more pilot workshops, it was becoming increasingly difficult for the universities to prove that their needs were similar to those more generally required:

> Now we have to prove that we are not the only one needing something, and that is not easy if we don't come together any more in workshops. The basic concepts seem to be fixed (based on past roll-in?), and 'sacred'. Everything that doesn't fit in is 'specific'. An example of this is timetables per programme and per stage. This is labelled as '[Low Country University] specific reporting issues', although we see them also on the websites of [Big_Civic] and [New Town universities].

The supplier was primarily concerned with the continued transferability of the module. This is in contrast to the pilots who, rather than simply demand a locally specific system, appear to require an application that is both local *and* global (cf. Williams 1997), both customized and a default:

> If from now on they only talk separately to each university and look for solutions for their specific situation, my fear remains that we will all end up with separate products, and we can start planning a 'back to the standard' project after a couple of years.

In other words, they want a system that matches their current practices but at the same time they are increasingly aware that to end up with 'separate products' would be counterproductive. Would their customized version be supported? Could they make use of later upgrades? The answer, they feared, would be no, and thus they began to look for commonalties across their practices by checking websites, holding discussions during testing sessions, and so on.

Here we see how the development of the student module has moved the discussion of the identity of the university from one where the issue was simply the extent to which universities were different from other organizations more generally, to one where the question concerns the differences among universities themselves? And, indeed, once they were thinking in terms of the higher education sector, there was a further shift where they recognized the increasing need to identify similarities among the group of universities participating in the development of the system.

Conclusion

The extent to which universities are similar to, or different from, other organizations has been the principal issue governing this chapter. We have attempted to show how it is not simply a question of identifying *a priori* a set of characteristics and elements which set universities apart, although this is the way that it is often portrayed in the literature (cf. Lockwood 1985; Heiskanen *et al.* 2000). Rather, through examining how a computer system designed with commercial organizations in mind is made to fit within the context of a university, we have shown how some of the differences and similarities are actively constructed and brought into being.

Moreover, we have emphasized the antagonistic, as well as contingent, nature of this process – i.e. the extent to which the successful realization of differences and similarities depends on the struggles of various actor networks – using notions such as translation and biography. We have described the ways in which aspects of Big_Civic's identity, role and working practices are taken or translated towards the system. In some respects this is in accordance with the initial goals of the pro-vice-chancellor in charge of the project, who wanted to make the university less organizationally specific through importing 'best business practice'. There is an increasing pressure to rethink many of the existing procedures and concepts according to new business process terms and Enterprise terminology even when such a process causes confusion and irritation.

We have also described the ways in which Enterprise is expanded and brought closer to universities. This occurred where there was recognition of the specificity of universities, the ways in which they are different from other organizations, such as those identified during processes of customization. However, the extent to which this uniqueness could be realized was also difficult to ascertain: Enterprise threw up so many 'demands for policy', that implementation decisions were never properly discussed, and change often occurred, therefore, through a process of default. Such customization as Enterprise could encompass, moreover, was increasingly moving to the level of the sector: a university's specifics would be incorporated only if they could be proved to be common to all (which was becoming increasingly difficult). Finally, even where differences were articulated and measures were taken to ensure that these were recognized within the system, it seemed that the system was often unable to shake off its history (i.e. students are much like employees on a training course, aren't they?).

In conclusion, the practices, procedures and processes being laid down with the introduction of these new forms of management and administration system have important consequences for the way in which the university is being reconfigured, and particularly the way in which certain important relationships are being developed. It would seem that the form of organization that is emerging, now that the Enterprise system has been adopted, and coupled with the pressures both to update and review internal processes and technologies in the light of upgrades and new modules, and to respond to the needs of other universities (who also make demands upon the system's future shape), is simply very different from how we might once have imagined conventional university structures and the processes that govern them.

It is well known that information and communications technologies provide powerful incentives for standardization, as well as the renegotiation of internal and external linkages in this way (cf. Chapter 4; Agre 2000a). Universities, if they are to make the most of standardized software, must, while resisting such pressures, learn how to manage these complicated *translation* processes. We wonder, to use the sentiments expressed by one member of the implementation team excited by the future possibilities that the system might offer, to what extent Big_Civic is beginning to think that its uniqueness is centred on the fact *that it now has an Enterprise system*.[9]

Notes

1. Another way of looking at this, following Powell and DiMaggio (1991), might be to suggest that there were various pressures towards institutional isomorphism.
2. By this he means the way a technology is developed in one context, and the processes and mechanisms by which it is diffused for use in other settings. For instance, a piece of software designed for one client may be 'packaged' and incorporated for general release as one component of a supplier's offering.
3. Davenport (1998), for instance, investigating a number of large corporations, describes how one company had developed a practice of giving its most important customers preferential treatment, which included sometimes shipping them products that had already been allocated to other accounts. Under the ERP system, however, it no longer had the flexibility to process orders in this way (see also Walsham 2001)
4. The version of the human resources and finance modules adopted by Big_Civic, for instance, embody aspects that are already specific to higher education institutions, and during the implementation these modules will be further tailored to meet local conditions.
5. As an aside, it could be argued that certain issues suffered from their place on the agenda: while those on the top were heavily debated, those lower down received only scant attention. What we are witnessing here is the organizing power of the agenda; and agenda setting is, of course, a foundational activity within universities (cf. Lockwood 1985). See Boden (1994) for a discussion of the role of the agenda more generally in organizations.
6. Interview with project administrator.
7. For a discussion of the identity of students, see Silver and Silver (1997).
8. Such is the confusion that laughter breaks out and one participant exclaims how all of this is beginning to 'sound like a philosophy class!'

9. This was an observation from one project team meeting where the discussion centred on the current review of the student office, where the registrar (and others) were carrying out research to compare themselves with the practices and procedures in student offices elsewhere. For one member of the project team this seemed nonsensical: 'What they are doing is looking at other universities, but it will not be accurate because we have [Enterprise and the Student Module] and no other [British] university has that – we are unique!'

8

Campus Management
and the Self-service Student

For students, self-service functions improve the quality of information and ease
the burden on administrative staff. Instead of having to wait for appointments
and documents in long lines by the financial aid and admissions offices, students
will be able to access a wide variety of services at Campus Management's
electronic kiosks (intranet) or from their residence hall via the Internet.
Additional services will also be provided, for example, students can apply
for on-campus housing, request additional balances on their tuition, inquire
about their current academic standing and look-up faculty changes for current
classes – all over the intranet.

(Supplier brochure)

Introduction

There is a growing body of work within science and technology studies that
argues that social theory plays a crucial role in the design of technology.
According to this view, engineers, innovators, technical specialists and the
like are not simply concerned with the production of new artefacts and
systems but will typically assume or construct a particular theory of society
or social relations which new technologies can be inserted into (cf. Callon
1986a, Latour 1996). Such theory can be (and often is) radical, ranging
from engineers depicting large-scale social change, such as widespread shifts
in consumption patterns, through to the characteristics of the users of the
future technologies (cf. Akrich 1992).[1] It is well known, too, that software
suppliers engage in similar strategies when designing new systems and that
such work involves the imagining and production of roles and identities of
future users as much as the writing of computer code. We seek to deploy
this form of thinking while describing the design and rollout of a new
student management system – the Campus Management module which we
met in the previous chapter.

Campus Management assumes the existence of a certain kind of user,
one that is seemingly appropriate for the various challenges facing modern
universities, but that does not as yet exist within universities. To bring him
or her into being will require radical changes in thinking and organization.

We say radical because the idea is to allow the traditionally 'passive' objects of administrative computer systems, students, to become the 'active' users. The students' use of Campus Management will be on a 'self-service' basis and they will be able to view and in some cases modify administrative and financial information about themselves and their courses. Self-service forms part of a set of thinking, we might even say philosophy, which the system supplier is attempting to develop and deploy alongside its software. These are not wholly new ideas but are ones borrowed from the world of electronic commerce. As such they raise important questions for universities, who will have to rethink some foundational and cherished responsibilities and relationships, and for institutional managers who will be forced to question the extent to which technologies (and their associated organizational philosophies) can be straightforwardly transferred across realms or sectors.

First, at the level of institutional management, one implication of Campus Management is that it will demand the renegotiation of the status of students and their relationship to the university. It is not only that students will be taking on new data inputting tasks, a job currently done by university staff, but in some cases they will also be responsible for the timeliness and accuracy of the data contained in their student record. We describe how Campus Management generates a number of contrasting reactions and objections from the different elements of the campus community, forcing university managers to rethink their plans. Much resistance comes, rather surprisingly, from those closest to the project – Campus Management's own steering committee. Through attending to this resistance it is possible to explore in some detail how the notion of self-service fits with existing conceptions and understandings of student role and identity.

Second, at the level of technology management, Campus Management signifies a new venture for Big_Civic University, which is unlike its previous experiences with organizational computer systems. Campus Management, as we have seen in Chapter 7, is to be a 'global product', and as such is designed to meet the needs and demands of many institutions from around the world. This has important implications for Big_Civic and its freedom to determine the shaping of its structures, processes and practices. We show, for instance, that, because of the university's involvement in and reliance on a network of other adopters and the system supplier, self-service functionality can be difficult to reject outright.

The arguments discussed here exemplify Chapter 3's concern for the ways in which work in the virtual university is continually made mobile (i.e. moving work from staff to students). It also builds on Chapter 5's interest in the way students are redescribed in terms of their roles and duties towards information. And, finally, it furthers Chapter 6's discussion of standardized computer systems and how they embody different modes of working from the ones commonly found in universities.

Self-service: where did the concept come from?

The notion of self-service first became popular in academic circles as a result of the work of Jonathan Gershuny who, in *After Industrial Society? The Emerging Self-service Economy* (1978), contradicted the firmly held belief that industrialized countries were becoming 'service economics'. His counterargument was that people were not in fact purchasing more services, but rather that consumers were investing in durable goods (such as washing machines, cars, vacuum cleaners, etc.) that would allow them to produce and consume services for *themselves*. Self-service principles, as he saw it, were set to spread elsewhere (leading to the growth of what he described as a 'post service' economy). One only has to look to the world of banking and the near universal usage of technologies such as automatic teller machines (ATMs) to see self-service in action (cf. Moon and Frei 2000; Gilster 2001). Today, self-service has become an important, albeit implicit, part of many of the 'dis-intermediation' arguments surrounding the growth of the Internet. Dis-intermediation, to paraphrase Agre (1999), might be understood as the increasing obsolescence of many of the institutional and organizational processes that play a mediating role between buyer and seller, borrower and lender, students and knowledge, and so on, such that it is said that anyone can connect to anyone else with minimal effort.

While much interest has focused on the various institutional and organizational mechanisms that are being reconfigured and (arguably) bypassed as a result of the Internet, there has been no study (at least none that we know of) that has worked through in detail the notion of self-service, and just what this might mean for institutions, organizations and their relationship to customers, employees, students, etc. This is, thus, both an important and a growing topic. For example, it has been estimated that around 60 per cent of all US organizations use some form of self-service technology to enable employees to access and maintain some part of their own human resource record. Interestingly, it is not simply that self-service is seen to have economic benefits through easing basic administration processes but they are also described as having an emancipatory aspect. According to some suppliers and commentators, having direct access to personal data is seen to 'empower' employees and give them greater 'control' over their careers:

> The Employee Self Service solution consists of a set of easy-to-use applications that empower employees to view, create, and maintain confidential personal data over an intranet or the Internet.
>
> (SAP brochure)

It's no secret that most companies introduce self-service technology for one primary reason: It can save huge sums of money by eliminating unwieldy processes that devour time and resources. Of course, other benefits can result from employees taking control of their own transactions, including helping them take greater responsibility and ownership of their careers.

(Greengard 1998: 2)

University self-service

This form of thinking (along with the cost saving and emancipatory rhetoric) has been transferred directly into higher education and has influenced organizational change strategies and computer systems implementations. Universities, perhaps more than other large public institutions, are seen to benefit from self-service technologies.[2] There is, for example, a growing and increasingly computer literate student population with access to extensive computer resources, both on campus and increasingly at home (see, for example, Crook 2002). Added to this is an increasingly stretched institutional and administrative resource (Hansen 1995). Institutional managers have also responded to the potential. Along with Campus Management, we know of several other self-service projects under way both in the UK and abroad. Two of particular note were conducted at Liverpool and Bath. Liverpool John Moores University (JMU), for instance, as part of a funded Joint Information Systems Committee (JISC) research project, recently added a 'self-service front end' to an existing legacy student record system. Bath University has also invested heavily in a new 'off the shelf' system that allows students to register online. Members of both projects have a well-defined vision of what they think self-service might do for their institution.

We met and talked with some of the technical people involved with implementing these technologies. We also attended conferences where they have given papers outlining their thinking and strategies. One project manager, for instance, described how the impetus for their system stemmed directly from his vice-chancellor who saw self-service as 'empowering the students to manage their own learning more actively', and how the system was 'for students' and 'not about students'. Another project manager, in contrast, did not see self-service as part of a student-centred educational philosophy but more as a reflection of a wider societal, business and technological shift to self-service formats (e.g. ATMs, Internet shopping). In his view, the Internet and computer systems like enterprise resource planning (ERP) systems, offer universities a new way of 'doing business', where there is a 'defined set of rules' that have the potential to radically reshape university structures and to make them 'more like other organizations'. Drawing on a banking commercial and Internet analogy, he is also well aware of the potential for self-service to reshape the role and identity of students:

> If we say that we want students to perform these actions for us [i.e. to self-administer], and because they do these things for us, we have to treat them in a different way. It is similar to the example of 'Smile' banking and the way they are blurring the boundary between 'customer' and 'cashier'.

The suggestion that self-service will complicate traditional relationships is an important one and brings us on to our discussion of Big_Civic and the take-up of the Campus Management module. What we intend to describe are attempts to move a university rooted in a conventional approach to student management, where students are administered directly by staff, to an institution made up of new electronic processes, where students have responsibilities towards conducting their own administration.

Building a new student–university relationship

The Campus Management module will handle data concerning the management and administration of students. It is being built by the large German software house SAP and implemented at Big_Civic University as well as at a number of other universities around the world. There are several features that make Campus Management interesting for study. First, Big_Civic is the first to go live with the system, and, along with a number of other pilots and early adopters, Big_Civic has been actively involved in its shaping. Second, the new student software is being installed at Big_Civic as one module in the context of an ERP system and there are plans to merge the module with existing ERP Finance and Human Resource modules, giving Big_Civic the 'first university ERP solution world-wide'. Third, also of interest is the fact that before embarking upon the project the system supplier had no previous knowledge or experience of implementing systems in a university setting. SAP's software, which was initially conceived for manufacturing firms, is seen as the *de facto* standard for the replacement of legacy systems in large commercial organizations (see Chapter 7).

Students are a particularly interesting category of computer systems user for a number of reasons. Academic and support staff have traditionally mediated students' relationship to administrative computer systems. Under Campus Management, however, students are to move from being passive objects of administration to one of the main groups of active users. In doing so they will be expected to do many different things for themselves: they will self-register for certain aspects of their degree course; they will validate the accuracy of other information (e.g. academic results, financial status and so on); and eventually students will be able to pay bills online; book accommodation; schedule meetings with their tutors, and so on – all without coming onto the campus. All of this will entail large-scale work at the level of software and institution.

In terms of software, Campus Management is not new software but a reworked version of the Training and Events Management module, a system used to run internal training programmes within commercial organizations. The module is structured around commercial categories such as supplier, employee and customer, and there was no notion of 'the student' within the system. The category of self-service student will, therefore, have to be created within the software. This, as we saw in the previous chapter, is a difficult process.

Just as this new category will have to be created within the software, it will simultaneously have to be created within the institution. Here again, the process is not straightforward. The relationship of the institution of the university to students has always been (and continues to be) a complex one. Over time it has been characterized as something akin to the relationship an apprentice might have with his or her master. In the same vein, a student has been seen as a ward of the university, placed there by parents or society. More recently, students have been as members (albeit junior ones) of the institution, with rights to serve on committees and in some cases help shape university decision making. Today they are commonly viewed as an institution's 'customers' or as the 'consumers' of higher education (Silver and Silver 1997). Despite the prominence of this latter view, we would argue that no one relationship appears to fully dominate and that the legacy or traces of previous relationships are still found within many universities. If we are correct about this, it begs the question as to how self-service might fit within this rather ambivalent relationship. Below we describe two facets of attempts to reconfigure the student–university relationship (the creation of new expectations concerning registration processes and responsibilities towards information) and we note some of the tensions that arise as the various legacies butt up against each other.

Queuing and confusion

As we mentioned in Chapter 5, there is a widespread recognition within Big_Civic that many of the processes relating to student management and administration are badly in need of updating. This accords with a feeling within higher education more generally that yearly enrolment or registration processes, for instance, where students are forced to queue for hours in large halls to complete paperwork that could be completed elsewhere (i.e. via a computer on campus or even at home over the Internet prior to travelling to university) are no longer acceptable. 'Queuing and confusion' is seemingly such a commonplace that some even describe it as an essential part of university life or as an important facet of 'becoming a student' (Gledhill 1999: 8). At Big_Civic, as elsewhere, however, there was an increasing awareness that such frustrations should be minimized given the changing demands of students as 'critical consumers'. An internal document outlines this reorientation and move to a 'service culture':

> Student tuition charges, possible top-up fees and vouchers are fuelling increased student expectations and prompting the move to a service culture. Students are no longer willing to stand in long queues to register or order transcripts nor are they happy to travel between different offices across the campus to deal with programme registration,

housing applications or payment of fees. Universities that can offer these functions (and others) on-line via self-service to an integrated information system will gain a competitive advantage.

(Internal report of the Student Management Strategy Group
to Management Information Development Service Spending
Authority, April 2000)

What is being articulated here are concerns for consumerism that according to Silver and Silver (1997) have been typical of American higher education since the 1970s and that have been increasingly appearing on UK campuses since the late 1990s. There is no need to rehearse this debate in any great detail as the implications of this trend are well and widely understood (though we return to this issue below). It is sufficient to say that one important aspect relevant to our discussion is that students as customers are now commonly seen to have new rights. According to Silver and Silver (1997), these can be described as 'the delivery of services promised', 'appropriate forms of services' and a 'greater access to information'. What is important to note is that self-service access appears to correspond with the need to fulfil these rights. At Liverpool, for instance, the project is described as helping decrease the administrative burden on staff (particularly academic staff) as well as 'improving services for students' (a system 'for' students and not 'about' students).[3] At Big_Civic, while there was a desire to improve the delivery of services, there was a particular emphasis on achieving this through encouraging access to, and ownership of, information.

Ownership of information

A common complaint throughout Big_Civic was that because no single person or department had 'ownership' of information, those inputting data were not overly concerned with its accuracy. This was increasingly important given the new demands placed upon the university to accurately report and manage its activities (see Chapter 5) as well as provide efficient services for its students. The resolution of this problem appeared to reside with self-service technologies and shifting responsibility for the ownership of data to those who could ensure its accuracy – the students. This view is by no means restricted to Big_Civic and can be found in a good practice guide to institutional management in higher education:

The best systems ensure that those who need to rely on the data are also those responsible for ensuring the accuracy of the data: it is of little use if, for example, entry of student fee information is a low priority for that part of the institution which enters it, or if, on the other hand, tutors who need accurate course and module lists feel that it is not their responsibility to take registers of attendance. This 'ownership' of the data is crucial.

(Gledhill 1999: 88)

Gledhill argues that in terms of student information, the best 'owners' are seen to be students themselves as 'they have most to lose if their records are wrong, and ought to be placed in a position not only to change any inaccurate data easily but also to be required to ensure that they are changed' (1999: 88). The suggestion is that students should become 'responsible' for the accuracy of *all* information the university might hold about them. Similar sets of aims were driving Campus Management. The university's Communication and Information Strategy, for instance, includes the following objective:

> To provide staff and students with access to information *appropriate to their needs* by a wide variety of information sources . . . All information should have owners who are responsible for up-to-date accuracy of that information.
>
> (italics in original)

In a further discussion document concerning Campus Management it is described how students could and should have direct, read access to their 'own personal and academic data'. On top of this, it is suggested that students should be able to input and modify data and that they, therefore, be given: 'write access to all self-service functions, including applications for admission, changes of address, module registration, leave of absence'. Interestingly, the tentative and preliminary nature of the suggestion that students should be allowed write access is highlighted by a question mark, which follows the suggestion. Such tentativeness is also present later in the document where it outlines some possible future scenarios for student registration:

> For Sept 2001, it is proposed that personal and module registration takes place in Departments via personal tutors. New students will attend first, check their personal details with their tutors and select module options where appropriate. Exactly how this is done depends upon the level of access to the system in Depts (and on the preference of the Dept):
>
> Option 1) If all tutors had access, e.g. via MySAP.Com and a web browser, it would be possible to call up the student details on screen, check/amend master data and select modules without the need to print, distribute and complete registration forms and module selection forms (and then re-input the data into the student system).
>
> Option 2) SAP provides student self-service via a web browser to carry out personal and module registration. New students could follow Option 1 with returning students carrying out their own registration after first meeting with their tutor. This could be carried out via selected clusters [of university PCs] or departmental PCs. Students could be made entirely responsible for ensuring that they register correctly and that their data are accurate or students could enter data under the supervision of central or local administrative or academic staff. With

students entering data, staff time could be used more productively in providing services for the students.

Providing students with direct access to the system is an issue that has raised some discussion within Big_Civic. Below we consider some of the debate that ensued among those groups who were responsible (directly and indirectly) for Campus Management's implementation.

Counteracting the sponsors group

The day-to-day management of the project was controlled by a small project team or 'sponsors group', which reported to a larger steering committee or 'strategy group'. Whereas the sponsors group was staffed by those actively involved in implementing Campus Management, the strategy group was made up of senior academics and non-academics who held full-time positions in other departments and would come together only every five or six weeks. The role of the strategy group, which was chaired, attended and minuted by members of the sponsors group, was ultimately to review progress, oversee potential problems, help coordinate the system rollout across the institution, and have the final say over the various technical and organizational issues that arose. In practice, however, the strategy group often acted as something of an orthogonal group (cf. Knorr-Cetina 1999). That is, it openly attempted to counteract the dynamics and power structures of the group it was charged with supervising. While the sponsors group was a narrowly focused body with strong investments in the Campus Management technology, the strategy group had a much wider membership, some of whom were openly critical of the project and its far-reaching objectives.

Objections ranged from those questioning the implications of self-service for foundational relationships and responsibilities, to the more practical issues of managing self-service access. One member, for instance, thought that self-service went far beyond the question of administrative procedures, to the nature of the university's relationship to its students, and this raised an issue about the way in which the system might undermine longstanding pastoral responsibilities. For instance, if a web browser or portal were to replace conventional mechanisms for the payment of accommodation bills etc., this would then increase or, worse still, force credit card use among students, thereby encouraging them to enter further networks of debt. Should the university be seen to be encouraging such practices?

Concerns were also expressed over whether students actually wanted or, more importantly, could be trusted with such access. This issue of trusting students is recognized as a more general problem. To return to the good practice guide mentioned earlier, Gledhill tackles a similar issue and suggests that, for academic matters and for many administrative matters, students should *not* be given direct, write access to a system as there is the potential for fraudulent use.[4] At Big_Civic the worry was not so much about fraudulent use as about whether students could be persuaded to update their own records. One department head, for instance, described how they currently had a problem with postgraduates failing to register changes in modules and

> If, as is suggested with the self-service option, the departmental student office no longer has responsibility for this data it is unclear what will persuade students to update their files electronically.
>
> (Internal memo)

What really troubled some members of the strategy group, perhaps more than these conceptual questions, was the rather technical issue of data access, i.e. how they were going to organize and manage the level of access that various users had to the system, their ability to view, input and update personal and course information. From the outset it was clear that deciding access rights held important implications and it was thus decided that several members should split from the group to form a smaller data access committee to tackle these basic issues before reporting back.

The task of working out access was potentially enormous. There was the issue of whether students should have the same access to the system regardless of the type of course they were following (some medical students, for instance, were simultaneously enrolled on the degree programme of a neighbouring university). Did the year they were in make a difference (i.e. would first-year students have the skills and wherewithal to complete their own registration)? Would the fact they were full-time or part-time, following a traditional degree course or a shorter lifelong learning module, a student studying on campus or a distance-learning student, and so on, make a difference? The method by which such issues could be resolved within the system was by allocating users with appropriate user or authorization profiles. An internal document describes these profiles in more detail:

> Access to the SAP Campus Management System is assigned by associating the user with an authorisation profile made up from a compilation of activities, which the profile allows the user to carry out. Users have common activity groups assigned to them rather than unique profiles. Each activity group restricts the data and transactions accessible to each user within that group.

However, rather than debate the merits of each case and decide on the appropriate user profiles, it was suggested to the group that these profiles be kept as 'simple as possible':

> Authorisation management will be a major business issue for the implementation of SAP Campus Management. Currently, we have over 2000 different profiles for SAP Finance and HR. This has a significant impact: a) on the administration and maintenance of SAP authorisations (setting up new staff etc.) which is in danger of using more than 1 FTE [full-time employee] of support time; b) on the performance of the system. The advice from [Computing Support] is that authorisations (and

consequently, the user profiles) should be planned as soon as possible and that they should be kept as simple as possible.

In other words, the worry is that developing and maintaining authorization profiles of several thousand students and staff will be prohibitive. Therefore in order to keep development and maintenance costs down, the suggestion from this group is both to limit access and, where access is granted, to keep this to as basic a level as possible.

More generally, then, it appeared that concerns were growing among the strategy group. There were many unknowns (whether or not they could realistically develop and manage profiles for students, whether students would respond favourably to, or could be trusted with, such access, etc.). A further important factor was that the supplier was late in delivering the latest version of the software, which meant that there would be little time for testing before the go-live date. The strategy group decided to postpone its decision on the issue until such time as there might be more 'certainty' surrounding the system. In the meantime, if the Campus Management implementation were to proceed, then it must do so in a much less adventurous manner, without self service functionality. This meant that Campus Management, rather than radically change the university, would instead mirror many of the current student management processes.

This was obviously a disappointment to the sponsors group who had invested much time and effort in developing the self-service concept across the university. At an away-day meeting, the pro-vice-chancellor in charge of the project described this postponement in terms of the strategy group's aversion to 'risk':

> The Strategy Group didn't want students doing self-registration or registration via the Web . . . [Therefore] the message given to SAP is that we want to minimize risk and minimize change. The screens will be different but overall business process will be the same. The Strategy Group consensus was risk averse.

The American model of the student

As we have already mentioned and partially discussed in Chapter 7, several other universities were involved as pilot sites in the design and development of Campus Management. One other pilot – an American university we shall call Large_Campus – was planning, along with Big_Civic, to be the first to go live with the system. Unlike its UK partner, however, this institution appeared to be enthusiastically embracing the technology. Indeed, not only was it open to the possibilities that self-service might afford but it was also attempting to persuade the supplier to incorporate further advanced functionality, such as credit card payment facilities and customer relationship management (CRM) software. While there has been little academic research carried out on administrative practices on US campuses, anecdotal evidence suggests that these technologies suit their more 'competitive' and 'market-oriented' admission processes as well as the mode of interaction they are attempting to establish with their students:

> With each passing year, [Large_Campus] students are becoming more and more proficient in their use of the Internet. One evidence of this is the increasing number of accesses to online services for students . . . from the campus website. Students can register through the web, check grades and even find out about holds and accounts information.
>
> (Online document)

The worry at Big_Civic now that it had 'temporarily' rejected self-service, was that it would lose its influence over the design of Campus Management. According to the pro-vice-chancellor, this is exactly what was happening with the American university's requests for CRM software. As he saw it, the other pilots were making requests for functionality that would not fit Big_Civic's existing processes:

> [Large_Campus] also plonked on the table more requests for CRM and that has blown the whole thing apart. If SAP meets this request, then that is less for us. SAP has finite support and [Large_Campus's] need is more complicated than ours is. If they are going to go live with a CRM approach and we're going for a 'handicraft' approach based on our more 'handicraft' and 'paper-based' approach then this has an implication for our business processes.

Even though Big_Civic had already decided that such technologies were incompatible with its pastoral responsibilities as well as its more 'handicraft' and 'paper-based' registration processes, both sets of needs could not be reconciled within Campus Management. The supplier has had to prioritize one set of requirements over another, choosing, as some internal critics have described, to build the system according to the needs of the larger US market. The worry now was that a system heavily favouring the US model of student administration would have implications for Big_Civic's own methods for managing students.

Indeed, this had already begun to happen in various places throughout the system where the university had to accommodate software designed for the other pilots, and this was having a detrimental effect on Big_Civic's functioning. One example (and there were many others) was software for recording applications by prospective students, which included some notable differences from the UK application process. As applicants to US universities are required to submit application fees, the system automatically generates an accounting record for each prospective student. In UK institutions there is no similar fee, therefore Big_Civic was left with the problem of having either to 'store' some 30,000 unwanted records each year (drastically slowing the system and hindering goals of efficiency and data redundancy), or to undertake local customization to avoid this, but potentially compromising later upgrades.

Conclusion

We have discussed attempts to build both a new software module within Big_Civic and a new kind of user – the self-administering student. Both aspects had initially received a good response. Generally there appeared to be much enthusiasm for the introduction of the new systems, particularly in those more paper-based and time-consuming functions for administering staff and students. There was also a recognition that processes for registering students were badly in need of updating; forcing students to queue for hours to complete paperwork that might be completed online was seen to be unacceptable, especially given the changing demands of students who were increasingly 'technologically literate' and 'critical as consumers'. However, there were also concerns that Campus Management could upset relationships. Some within the strategy group were sceptical of the proposal to grant self-service access to students. This was not only because there were issues of further organizational change but also because Campus Management went far beyond the question of administrative procedures to the nature of the university's relationship to its students, and this raised concerns about the way in which the system might undermine longstanding pastoral responsibilities. The university, it seemed, while ready for the system was not yet ready for self-service.

However, towards the latter stages of the project, Big_Civic had to accept functionality designed for other universities. This process of closure had developed around the system as the supplier was finding it difficult to incorporate all of the demands of the pilots. Campus Management is, after all, a global product. To what extent this means that Big_Civic will eventually be forced to adopt self-service functionality or that its processes will come further to resemble those of other institutions is as yet unclear – at the time of writing the implementation is still under way. However, the fact that these types of technologies are readily available is bound to become a factor shaping future discussions and decisions concerning student management. For instance, in one particular strategy group meeting, on learning that the system generated a record to capture the application fee, one of the members made the suggestion: 'why don't we charge a fee for every application?' It was several brief moments before the others seated around the table realized that he was joking. For just a split second, however, it was a serious item on the table, worthy of consideration.

Notes

1. In his description of the design and building of an 'electric car' by French engineers during the 1970s, for instance, Callon (1986a) argues that this work was premised on the belief that society was on the brink of shifting its preference for combustion engines to more environmentally friendly battery-powered alternatives. While on this occasion the engineers were proved 'wrong', their

theorizing was still a central factor in the shaping and eventual outcome of this project.

2. See Bellamy and Taylor's (1998) discussion of technological change under way in local government, where parallels can be drawn between what is happening in universities and similar changes under way in processes to manage the citizen–government relationship. Under the auspices of the UK's E-Government agenda, a number of suppliers have recently begun to promote customer relationship management (CRM) software (and self-service solutions) to public administration offices: a process that, if adopted, will lead to a reinvention of the 'citizen'.

3. Interestingly, the Liverpool project posted an 'evaluation report' on its website, where success factors as well as some of the technical and organizational difficulties experienced are described. It points to instances where self-service systems have had unexpected outcomes and even the reverse effects to those originally anticipated. Rather than decrease staff involvement in student administration, for instance, academics were drawn further into the process, being automatically emailed by the system each time a student registered for a course, meaning that at certain periods they were forced to deal with hundreds of emails.

4. His suggestion, alternatively, is that students should be made responsible for checking their data and having it changed by the appropriate staff.

9

Reflection and Conclusion

We described in the introduction to this book how the dominant message among commentators on higher education appears to be that the university, as an institution, is in crisis; it is to use Readings' much publicized phrase a 'ruined institution' (1996). One element of this crisis, according to the influential writer Ronald Barnett (2000), is that because of increasing pressures to engage with new constituencies, audiences, knowledges, standards and purposes, the university is losing its specificity and 'uniqueness' – the very things that once set it apart from other organizations. In spite of the lack of an empirical base, many commentators seem to agree that new information and communications technologies (ICTs), and especially the Internet, are a significant element in accentuating, if not actually causing, this current condition.

We wholeheartedly support the thesis that the institution of the university is changing in fundamental ways, and that these changes deserve to be analysed both in more detail than they have to date and in different ways. But, we take issue with those more causal arguments that typically accompany the introduction of new technologies. They often ignore the individual dynamics of technologies and talk as if there were no ground or terrain to be travelled between the present institution and some future end-state: as if, in other words, there were no 'layers' between an institution and its goals and information technology policies. This book, in contrast, has emphasized the complexity of the process of *putting* the university online. In so doing, our focus has been somewhat different from conventional studies of universities.

What is more, we have also argued for new ways of seeing the relationship between technologies and universities. We think there is little purchase when studying technology and institutions to concentrate simply on what is lost (e.g. what a technology proscribes) or, for that matter, what is gained. The focus ought instead to be on the processes by which an institution and technology mutually shape each other. To do so, we argue, is to gain a deeper understanding of just how new technologies are contributing to the reshaping of higher education and then, in turn, of how technologies are being shaped for use within universities.

There are three key topics stemming from the research presented here, each of which can be linked to one of the terms in the subtitle of the book: information, technology and organizational change.

Information

Throughout this book we have focused on how the university has been redefined in a number of new ways, one of which is in terms of the storage, processing, transmission and sharing of information. While perhaps anti-thetical to conventional understandings of higher education, it has, never-theless, become a powerful rhetoric in and around campuses. What interested us and guided the direction of much of the book is how this discursive reorientation was achieved. We have described at some length how *informa-tional discourses* have been used by institutional managers to redefine what the university is, what its problems are, and how these problems could and should be addressed (Chapter 5). All this has contributed to making the Internet and other technologies, to borrow a phrase from Clark and Fujimura (1992), appear as the 'right tools for the job' (see also Berg 1997). Once the university has been successfully described in terms of information, then, these technologies appear not only as important but also as essential to its future.

Should this general reorientation of the university concern us? Might it be argued that the view of the university as information downplays certain things while highlighting others? For instance, it contrasts with the campus-based notion of the university as a 'space of encounter' alluded to in Chapter 4. Related to this, should we be more concerned about the nature and types of information being collected and stored than about how and where it is communicated? There is, for instance, the information required to measure Readings' (1996) notion of the 'university of excellence', and then there is the very different type of information required to measure the 'university of culture', which is also described in his book. There are, as he reminds us, different ways of rendering an account, only some of which are recognizable to an accountant. Does the focus on the information actually obscure the more educationally significant process of informing?

A further theme we have highlighted is the processes of standardiza-tion associated with producing and maintaining this informational view of higher education. We have, for instance, gone to great lengths to articulate the various forms of heterogeneous engineering required to fit university practices to new technologies (and vice versa). In central administrations, we have seen pressures to reshape functions and practices according to the various process models embodied in enterprise software. At the level of the wider institution, we have seen pressures to replicate practices across depart-ments so that information (about student fees, new courses, etc.) is always 'consistent'. We have also witnessed how the introduction of technology has itself generated further unanticipated demands for standardization. In teaching, we have seen how the widespread availability of email across the student body has increased the need for commensurate forms of treatment in the assessment of essays. In Chapter 3, we described such standardization as the paradoxical concretization of what was once a highly 'virtual' organization. What are the implications of this for the university?

Standardization is a complex issue, and though it is seldom thought about in this way, it can lead to both homogenization *and* diversity (Agre 2000a). Systems like enterprise resource planning (ERP), by clarifying and making explicit the various roles and responsibilities within the university, may help future developments and increase experimentation in online learning and distance education by facilitating the complex processes of enrolling actors and resources required to implement these technologies (see Chapter 3). Alternatively, there are possible dangers if we standardize the 'wrong things'; if, as Phil Agre (2000a) suggests, we standardize those 'differences that make a difference'. In this respect, when replacing the administrative apparatus of the university, we risk destroying or submerging those interactions that are tacit, informal and flexible, the very processes that might, for instance, offer important forms of support to students, staff and others within the university. Self-service technologies, by shifting the burden of administration to students (on the model of electronic commerce – see Chapter 8) might actually jeopardize the university's relationship with its students. How, for instance, might a student ask for an extension on the payment of a late rent bill through a self-service portal? Is this simply a matter of 'functionality' just waiting to be built into the system? How will all the cases that do not quite fit, be supported? Alternatively, will 'nonstandard' requests simply fall between the inevitable cracks in the system?

Technology

Many of the 'negotiations' and 'struggles' that we have described throughout the various chapters of this book have resulted from basic temporal, spatial and process incommensurabilities between the technologies and the institution of the university. Such incommensurabilities, while not easily reconciled, provide us with important insights into the mutual shaping of technology and institution. In the Cyber Culture course described in Chapter 4, for instance, there was the issue of the gulf between a new virtual course available on the web and the campus-based course most students were familiar with. Interestingly, the team at North_Campus attempted to resolve this issue through giving the virtual courses a greater 'material presence' so that students, as they see it, might value both in the same way. The fascinating issue here is that the Cyber Culture module brings into focus for the team just how much work the campus currently undertakes for the university, and their attempts to *repair* what they see as a 'gap' between the technology and the university. Of course, what this suggests is that the university campus will continue to have relevance for those dedicated to putting the university online: it is, as Brown and Duguid (2000) propose, not simply a constraint, but a 'resourceful constraint'.

Let us now focus on generic and standard computer systems, where we see the clearest example of a gulf between the university and technology. Generally, the introduction of ERP systems into organizations provides for a dilemma: while adopters wish to capitalize on the benefits of standardized software, they will not want to suffer the costs of unwanted organizational change in adapting organizational processes to match those process models embedded in the software. For universities, this dilemma is more acute: while there are similarities between the workings of a university and those of other organizations, there are also significant differences, many of which are the result of longstanding institutional and academic traditions. The process of tailoring these systems to fit universities is therefore far from straightforward.[1] What we have argued is that aspects of the university are difficult to classify within the software. Below, we describe a number of points related to this classification problem.

One common problem is that, organizationally, universities, like many large institutions, do not know themselves well enough (see Chapter 7), and when presented with new systems such as ERP which are known to be highly prescriptive, are tempted to describe themselves according to the available language and process templates. There are a number of drawbacks to prescriptive systems, one important feature being that 'differences' are not described easily within these systems and thus tend to be ignored or thought of as unimportant. However, in the process of deployment it is frequently these supposedly unimportant differences that turn out to be the ones that 'make a difference' – they are not so unimportant after all.

A related problem is that there are 'fuzzy' boundaries between universities and organizations. Universities engage in many activities in the same way as any other organization does (the procurement of software, for instance), yet they are recognized by all (including, now, software suppliers) as 'something a bit different'. This makes the use of standard software all the more difficult. The depiction within the Campus Management module of students as 'special types of employees' and the subsequent tensions this provoked, suggests this is far from a trivial problem and one that will not go away.[2] The process of putting the university online, we suggest, will continue to highlight, as well as refashion, the boundaries between universities and other types of organization.

One outcome of this classification failure, if indeed 'failure' is the right word, is that universities will increasingly have to procure software as a 'community' or 'sector' in order to exert pressure on suppliers to build university-specific versions (e.g. Big_Civic's membership of the SAP Higher Education Research User Group). The consequences of this are obvious: from now on, the university will have to negotiate and struggle both with the supplier *and* with other higher education institutions. This suggests that there will be a tendency towards 'institutional isomorphism' (Powell and DiMaggio 1991; see also Chapter 8).

We were fortunate in the development of the Campus Management system to have witnessed such conflicts and pressures in the development process of what might in the future become the standard model of developing software within higher education. In the design of this new module, we saw how more attention was paid to the search for generalizable concepts than to the needs of individual institutions. We saw the system 'converge' on a particular design, not because the supplier had found the one 'best model' or set of practices but because this is the nature of standardized software and the production of a 'global product'.[3] This convergence, then, has important implications for the future shaping of institutional structures and processes of those who adopt such systems, and who will have to fit their university around such generalized concepts.[4] In summary, then, what we have seen are some of the ways in which putting the university online will directly and indirectly mediate the relationships between universities and software suppliers and between universities and other higher educational institutions around the world.

Organizational change

We might ask whether the university is organized to undergo such processes of change. Is it equipped to make use of new ICTs while retaining its foundational institutional values? Is the university necessarily losing its organizational specificity and uniqueness as it gears up to go online?

Certainly, the picture emerging is of computer systems and technologies that are reshaping the conventional processes and practices of universities. This is in some respects in accordance with the goals of the senior management teams at Big_Civic and City_Campus who, through their respective restructuring programmes, were attempting to make their universities less organizationally idiosyncratic and more 'corporate'. Yet much change, we argue, stems not from direct university or senior management policy but from adjustments to fit the university to the demands of the technology. The level of organizational change required to implement an ERP system within a university appeared to be substantially greater than any of the team could ever have anticipated. Moreover, this shaping also occurs in those places where the university is seemingly able to have most direction over the implementation – the customization process. Attempts to tailor ERP modules placed a strain on existing institutional structures, sometimes shifting the locus of decision making from established mechanisms to the more informal, loosely-based coalitions surrounding the implementation. The collegiate model of 'rule by committee' is at odds with the demands of integrated enterprise systems because they generate more issues than the part-time membership of such committees is able to deal with.

However, we would argue that it is not simply that the institution of the university is being pulled apart, as some commentators have suggested, or is losing its uniqueness (Barnett 2000). Rather, what we are witnessing is a new social, spatial, temporal and technical division of labour which requires new organizational practices and structures to undertake both the division and, what is not always well emphasized, the subsequent combination of the newly divided institution (Chapter 3). University staff are simultaneously engaged in negotiations and struggles to implement new technologies, to reconfigure these technologies in the light of features they perceive to be specific to the university, and to do much work reconfiguring the organization of the university. In other words, what we found was that, despite pressures to change, whether through conscious choice or 'default', the university also remains committed to many established structures, identities and relationships.

Conclusion: back to knowledge

What, in the end, is significant about the process of putting the university online? What is the most significant outcome of all the work described in this book? The obvious answer is that the process of putting the university online results in the online university. But as we have shown, this is not, or not unambiguously, the case. We think that things are more subtle than this. The important (and desirable) outcome of the process is a new kind of university. It is not, however, one that is distinguished from its former self in terms of technologies, structures or processes, but rather it differs in terms of its degree of self-knowledge. As universities have lost their monopoly of knowledge about the world, they have been offered a new opportunity, one that they have, perhaps surprisingly, traditionally spurned – knowledge about themselves.

Notes

1. See Paul Du Gay's *In Praise of Bureaucracy* (2000) for a similar discussion of the application of thinking and change processes from private enterprises to government offices.
2. See Bowker and Star's *Sorting Things Out: Classification and its Consequences* (1999) for a discussion of the persistence of such classification problems.
3. See Bowker (2000) for further elaboration of this point about convergence as it is applied to biodiversity informatics.
4. Of course, an adopter can always reshape the software, but, as we have described throughout the book, this can be difficult to do.

References

Abeles, T. (1998) The academy in a wired world, *Futures*, 30(7): 603–13.

Abeles, T.P. (1999) The inevitability of a business model for higher education, *Foresight: The Journal of Futures Studies, Strategic Thinking and Policy*, 1(1): 10–16.

Agre, P. (1999) Designing the new information services, *Educom Review*, 34(5): 12–14, 42–3.

Agre, P. (2000a) Infrastructure and institutional change in the networked university, *Information, Communication and Society*, 3(4): 494–507.

Agre, P. (2000b) Imagining the wired university. Paper presented at the Symposium on the Future of the University, University of Newcastle, September.

Akrich, M. (1992) The de-scription of technical objects, in W. Bijker and J. Law (eds) *Shaping Technology/Building Society*. Cambridge, MA: MIT Press.

Allen, D. and Wilson, T. (1996) Information strategies in UK higher education institutions, *International Journal of Information Management*, 6. 239–51.

Appadurai, A. (ed.) (1992) *The Social Life of Things: Commodities in Cultural Perspective*. Cambridge: Cambridge University Press.

Balderston, F. (1995) *Managing Today's University: Strategies for Viability, Change and Excellence*. San Francisco: Jossey-Bass.

Barnett, R. (2000) *Realizing the University in an age of super complexity*. Buckingham: SRHE/Open University Press.

Becker, H.S. (1982) *Art Worlds*. Berkeley, CA: University of California Press.

Bell, D. (1976) *The Coming of Post-industrial Society: A Venture in Social Forecasting*. London: Penguin.

Bellamy, C. and Taylor, J.A. (1998) *Governing in the Information Age*. Buckingham: Open University Press.

Beniger, J. (1986) *The Control Revolution: Technological and Economic Origins of the Information Society*. Cambridge, MA: Harvard University Press.

Berg, M. (1997) *Rationalizing Medical Work: Decision-support Techniques and Medical Practices*. Cambridge, MA: MIT Press.

Berg, M. and Timmermans, S. (1997) Orders and their others: on the constitution of universalities in medical work. Paper presented at the Actor Network and After Conference, Keele University, UK, 10–11 July.

Bijker, W. and Law, J. (eds) (1992) *Shaping Technology/Building Society: studies in socio-technical change*. Cambridge, MA and London: MIT Press.

Bloomfield, B. and Vurdubakis, T. (1994) Re-presenting technology: IT consultancy reports as textual reality constructions, *Sociology*, 28(2): 455–77.

Boden, D. (1994) *The Business of Talk: Organizations in Action*. Cambridge: Polity Press.

Boden, D. and Molotch, H.L. (1994) The compulsion of proximity, in R. Friedland and D. Boden (eds) *No(w)here: Space, Time and Modernity*. Berkeley, CA: University of California Press, pp. 257–86.

Bowker, G. (2000) Biodiversity datadiversity, *Social Studies of Science*, 30(5): 643–83.

Bowker, G. (1994) Information mythology: the world of/as information, in L. Bud-Frierman (ed.) *Information Acumen: The Understanding and Use of Knowledge in Modern Business*. London: Routledge, pp. 231–47.

Bowker, G. and Star, S.L. (1996) How things (actor-net)work: classification, magic and the ubiquity of standards. Graduate School of Library and Information Science, University of Illinois at Urbana-Champaign, at http://weber.ucsd.edu/~gbowker/pubs.htm (accessed 14 June 2002).

Bowker, G. and Star, S. (1999) *Sorting Things Out: Classification and its Consequences*. Cambridge, MA: MIT Press.

Brady, T., Tierney, M. and Williams, R. (1992) The commodification of industry applications software, *Industrial and Corporate Change*, 1(3): 489–514.

Brown, J.S. and Duguid, P. (1995) Universities in the digital age, available at http://www.parc.xerox.com/ops/members/brown/papers/university.html (accessed 13 May 2000).

Brown, J.S. and Duguid, P. (2000) *The Social Life of Information*. Boston: Harvard Business School Press.

Brown, S. and Capdevila, R. (1997) Perpetuum mobile: substance, force and the sociology of translation. Paper presented at the Actor Network and After Conference, Keele University, UK, 10–11 July.

Bull, G., Dallinga-Hunter, C., Epelboin, Y., Frackman, E. and Jennings, D. (1994) *Information Technology: Issues for Higher Education Management*. London: Jessica Kingsley Publishers.

Callon, M. (1986a) The sociology of an actor-network: the case of the electric vehicle, in M. Callon, J. Law and A. Rip (eds) *Mapping the Dynamics of Science and Technology*. London: Macmillan.

Callon, M. (1986b) Some elements of a sociology of translation: domestication of the scallops and the fishermen of St Brieuc Bay, in J. Law (ed.) *Power, Action and Belief: A New Sociology of Knowledge?* London: Routledge.

Callon, M. (1991) Techno-economic networks and irreversibility, in J. Law (ed.) *A Sociology of Monsters. Essays on Power, Technology and Domination*. London: Routledge, pp. 132–61.

Carrier, J. and Miller, D. (eds) (1998) *Virtualism: A New Political Economy*. Oxford: Berg.

Ciborra, C. (1999) Notes on improvisation and time in organisations, *Accounting, Management and Information Technologies*, 9: 77–94.

Ciborra, C. (2000) *From Control to Drift: The Dynamics of Corporate Information Infrastructures*. Oxford: Oxford University Press.

Clark, A. and Fujimura, J. (1992) *The Right Tools for the Job: At Work in the 20th Century Sciences*. Princeton: Princeton University Press.

CVCP (Committee of Vice Chancellors and Principals) (2000) *The Business of Borderless Education*. London: CVCP.

Cooper, R. and Law, J. (1995) Organization: distal and proximal views, *Research in the Sociology of Organizations*, 13: 237–74.

Cornford, J. (2000) The virtual university is the university made concrete, *Information, Communication and Society*, 3(4): 508–25.

Crook, C. (2002) Learning as cultural practice, in M.R. Lea and K. Nicoll (eds) *Distributed Learning: Social and Cultural Approaches to Practice*. London: RoutledgeFalmer.

Crook, C. and Barrowcliff, D. (2000) Ubiquitous computing on campus: patterns of engagement by university students, paper submitted to the *International Journal of Human Computer Interaction* (http://devpsy.lboro.ac.uk/psy/ckc/papers/ijhci.htm).

Cunningham, S., Tapsall, S., Ryan, Y., Stedman, L. *et al.* (1998) *New media and Borderless Education: A Review of the Convergence between Global Media Networks and Higher Education Provision*, Australian Government, Department of Employment, Education, Training and Youth Affairs, Evaluations and Investigations Programme, Higher Education Division. Available at http://www.deetya.gov.au/highered/eippubs/cip97-22/eip9722.pdf (accessed 14 June 2002).

Davenport, T. (1998) Putting the enterprise into the enterprise system, *Harvard Business Review*, 76(4): 121–32.

Davis, J. (1998) Scooping up vanilla ERP: off-the-shelf versus customised software, *InfoWorld*, 20(47): 1–4.

Du Gay, P. (2000) *In Praise of Bureaucracy: Weber, Organisation, Ethics*. London: Sage.

Gasser, L. (1986) The integration of computing and routine work, *ACM Transactions on Office Information Systems*, 4: 205–25.

Gershuny, J. (1978) *After Industrial Society? The Emerging Self-service Economy*. London: Macmillan.

Gibbons, M., Limoge, C., Nowotny, H., Schwartzman, S. *et al.* (1994) *The New Production of Knowledge: The Dynamics of Science and Research in Contemporary Societies*. London: Sage.

Gilster, P.A. (2001) Making online self-service work, *Workforce*, 80(1): 54–62.

Gladieux, L.E. and Swail, W.S. (1999) *The Virtual University and Educational Opportunity: Issues of Equity and Access for the Next Generation*. Washington, DC: The College Board.

Gledhill, J.M. (1999) *Managing Students*. Buckingham: Open University Press.

Goddard, A.D. and Gayward, P.H. (1994) MAC and the Oracle family: achievements and lessons learnt, *Axix*, 1(1): 45–50.

Goddard, J.B., Charles, D., Pike, A., Potts, G. and Bradley, D. (1994) *Universities and Communities*. London, CVCP.

Gordon, R. (2000) Does the 'new economy' measure up to the great inventions of the past? *Journal of Economic Perspectives*, 14(4): 49–74.

Green, S. and Harvey, P. (1999) Scaling place and networks: an ethnography of ICT 'innovation' in Manchester. Paper presented to the Internet and Ethnography Conference, University of Hull, UK, 13–14 December.

Greengard, S. (1998) Building a self-service culture that works, *Workforce*, 77(7): 60–9.

Grint, K. and Woolgar, S. (1997) *The Machine at Work: Technology, Organisation and Work*. Oxford: Polity/Blackwell.

Halliday, F. (1999) The chimera of the 'international university', *Foreign Affairs*, 75(1): 99–120.

Hammersley, M. and Atkinson, P. (1995) *Ethnography: Principles and Practice*, 2nd edn. London: Routledge.

Hansen, H.R. (1995) A case study of mass information systems, *Information and Management*, 28: 215–25.

Hanseth, O. and Braa, K. (1998) Technology as traitor: emergent SAP infrastructure in a global organisation, in R. Hirscheim, M. Newman and J.I. DeGross (eds) Proceedings of the Nineteenth International Conference on Information Systems, ICIS'98. Helsinki, December 1998, 188–97.

Hara, N. and Kling, R. (2000) Student distress in web-based distance education, *Information, Communication and Society*, 3(4): 557–79.

Harvey, D. (1987) *The Condition of Postmodernity: An Enquiry into the Origins of Cultural Change*. Oxford: Basil Blackwell.

HEFCE (Higher Education Funding Council for England) (1999) *Communications and Information Technology Materials for Learning and Teaching in HE and FE: Summary Report*, HEFCE report 99/60, October.

Heiskanen, A., Newman, M. and Simila, J. (2000) The social dynamics of software development, *Accounting, Management and Information Technologies*, 10: 1–32.

Hughes, T.P. (1986) The seamless web: technology, science, etcetera, etcetera, *Social Studies of Science*, 16: 281–92.

Hughes, T.P. (1983) *Networks of Power: Electrification in Western Society, 1880–1930*. Baltimore, MD: Johns Hopkins University Press.

JISC (1995) *Guidelines for Developing An Information Strategy*. Available at http://www.jisc.ac.uk/pub/infstrat/ (accessed 14 June 2002).

Johnston, S. (1999) Introducing and supporting change towards more flexible teaching approaches, in A. Tait and R. Mills (eds) *The Convergence of Distance and Conventional Education*. London: Routledge.

Kiesler, S. and Sproull, L. (1987) The social process of technological change in organizations, in S. Kiesler and L. Sproull (eds) *Computing and Change on Campus*. Cambridge: Cambridge University Press.

Kling, R., Crawford, H., Rosenbaum, H., Sawyer, S. and Weisband, S. (2000) *Learning from Social Information: Information and Communications Technologies in Human Contexts*. Centre for Social Informatics, Indiana University. Available at http://www.slis.indiana.edu/SI/Arts /SI_report_Aug_14.pdf (accessed 14 June 2002).

Knorr-Cetina, K. (1999) *Epistemic Cultures: How the Sciences Make Knowledge*. Cambridge, MA: Harvard University Press.

Koch, C. (1999) SAP R\3 – an IT plague or the answer to the tailor's dream?, working paper. Institute for Technology and Social Science, Technical University of Denmark.

Kopytoff, I. (1992) The cultural biography of things: commoditization as process, in A. Appadurai (ed.) *The Social Life of Things: Commodities in Cultural Perspective*. Cambridge: Cambridge University Press.

Kumar, K. (1997) The need for place, in A. Smith and F. Webster (eds) *The Postmodern University*. Buckingham: SRHE/Open University Press, pp. 27–35.

Latour, B. (1987) *Science in Action: How to Follow Scientists and Engineers through Society*. Harvard, MA: Harvard University Press.

Latour, B. (1988a) *The Pasteurization of France*. Cambridge, MA: Harvard University Press.

Latour, B. (1988b) The politics of explanation: an alternative, in S. Woolgar (ed.) *Knowledge and Reflexivity: New Frontiers in the Sociology of Knowledge*. London: Sage, pp. 155–76.

Latour, B. (1993) *We Have Never Been Modern*. London: Harvester Wheatsheaf.

Latour, B. (1996) *Aramis or the Love of Technology*. Cambridge, MA: Harvard University Press.

Law, J. (1987) Technology and heterogeneous engineering: the case of the Portuguese expansion, in W.E. Bijker, T.P. Hughes and T.J. Pinch (eds) *The Social Construction of Technical Systems: New Directions in the Sociology and History of Technology.* Cambridge, MA: MIT Press, pp. 111–34.

Law, J. (1994) *Organising Modernity.* Oxford: Blackwell.

Law, J. and Callon, M. (1995) Engineering and sociology in a military aircraft project: a network analysis of technological change, in S.L. Star (ed.) *Ecologies of Knowledge: Work and Politics in Science and Technology.* Albany: State University of New York Press.

Lockwood, G. (1985) Universities as organizations, in G. Lockwood and J. Davies (eds) *Universities: The Management Challenge.* Windsor: NFER/Nelson.

Lockwood, G. and Davies, J. (eds) (1985) *Universities: The Management Challenge.* Windsor: NFER/Nelson.

Lozinsky, S. (1998) *Enterprise-wide Software Solutions.* London: Addison-Wesley.

Mackenzie, D. and Wajcman, J. (eds) (1999) *The Social Shaping of Technology,* 2nd edn. Buckingham: Open University Press.

March, J. (1987) Old colleges, new technology, in S. Kiesler and L. Sproull (eds) *Computing and Change on Campus.* Cambridge: Cambridge University Press.

March, J. (1989) Exploration and exploitation in organizational learning, *Organizational Science,* 2(1).

Marchese, T. (1998) Not-so-distant competitors: how new providers are remaking the post-secondary market, *American Association for Higher Education Bulletin,* May: 16–20.

Markus, M., Axline, S., Petrie, D. and Tanis, C. (2000) Learning from adopters' experiences with ERP, *Journal of Information Technology,* 15: 245–65.

Mason, R. (1999) European trends in the virtual delivery of education, in G.M. Farrell (ed.) *The Development of Virtual Education: A Global Perspective.* Vancouver: Commonwealth of Learning, pp. 77–87.

Mackay, H., Carne, C., Beynon-Davies, P. and Tudhope, D. (2000) Reconfiguring the user: using rapid application development, *Social Studies of Science,* 30(5): 737–57.

McLaughlin, J., Rosen, P., Skinner, D. and Webster, A. (1999) *Valuing Technology: Organisations, Culture and Change.* London: Routledge.

McLoughlin, I.P. (1999) *Creative Technological Change: The Shaping of Technology and Organisation.* London: Routledge.

McNay, I. (1995) From the collegial academy to corporate enterprise: the changing cultures of universities, in T. Schuller (ed.) *The Changing University?* Buckingham: SRHE/Open University Press, pp. 105–15.

Middlehurst, R. (2001) University challenges: borderless higher education, today and tomorrow, *Minerva,* 39: 3–26.

Moon, Y. and Frei, F.X. (2000) Exploding the self-service myth, *Harvard Business Review,* 78(3): 26–30.

Newby, H. (1999) Higher education in the 21st century: some possible futures, discussion paper. CVCP: London.

Newman, R. and Johnson, F. (1999) Sites of power and knowledge? Towards a critique of the virtual university, *British Journal of Sociology of Education,* 20(1): 79–88.

Noam, E. (1995) Electronics and the dim future of the university, *Science,* 270(13): 247–9.

Noble, D.F. (1998) Digital diploma mills: the automation of higher education, *Science as Culture,* 7(3): 355–68.

OECD (Organization for Economic Cooperation and Development) (2000) *Is There A New Economy? First Report on the OECD Growth Project*. Paris: OECD.

Parker, M. and Jary, D. (1995) The McUniversity: organisation, management and academic subjectivity, *Organization*, 2(2): 319–38.

Parr, A. and Shanks, G. (2000) A model of ERP project implementation, *Journal of Information Technology*, 15: 289–303.

Pollock, N. (1998) Working-around a computer system: some aspects of a hybrid sociology. Unpublished PhD thesis, University of Lancaster, UK.

Pollock, N. (forthcoming) Mis-using the software or the tension of work-arounds: how programmers negotiate the use of a technology, *Science, Technology, and Human Values*. Submitted for publication.

Pollock, N. and Cornford, J. (2000) Theory and practice of the virtual university, *EASST Review*, 19(2): 9–11.

Porter, T.M. (1994) Information, power and the view from nowhere, in L. Bud-Frierman (ed.) *Information Acumen: The Understanding and Use of Knowledge in Modern Business*. London: Routledge, pp. 217–30.

Powell, W. and DiMaggio, P. (eds) (1991) *The New Institutionalism in Organizational Analysis*. Chicago: University of Chicago Press.

Rachel, J. and Woolgar, S. (1995) The discursive structure of the social-technical divide: the example of information systems development, *The Sociological Review*, 43(2): 251–73.

Readings, B. (1996) *The University in Ruins*. Cambridge, MA: Harvard University Press.

Ritzer, G. (1998) *The McDonaldization Thesis: Explorations and Extensions*. London: Sage.

Rudinow Saetnan, A. (1991) Rigid politics and technological flexibility, *Science, Technology, and Human Values*, 16(4): 419–47.

Schuller, T. (ed.) (1995) *The Changing University?* Buckingham: SRHE/Open University Press.

Scott, P. (ed.) (1998) *The Globalization of Higher Education*. Buckingham: SRHE/Open University Press.

Shore, C. and Wright, S. (1999) Audit culture and anthropology: neo-liberalism in British higher education. Unpublished mimeo, Goldsmiths College, London.

Silver, H. and Silver, P. (1997) *Students: Changing Roles, Changing Lives*. Buckingham: Open University Press.

Smith, A. and Webster, F. (eds) (1997) *The Postmodern University? Contested Visions of Higher Education in Society*. Buckingham: SRHE/Open University Press.

Star, S.L. and Ruhleder, K. (1996) Steps toward an ecology of infrastructure: design and access for large information spaces, *Information Systems Research*, 7(1): 111–34.

Stephens, K. (1999) Notes from the margins: library experiences of postgraduate distance-learning students, in A. Tait and R. Mills (eds) *The Convergence of Distance and Conventional Education*. London: Routledge.

Thompson, E. (1980) *Writing by Candlelight*. London: Merlin.

Tierney, M. and Williams, R. (1991) Issues in the black-boxing of technologies, PICT working paper no. 22. Edinburgh: University of Edinburgh.

Trigg, R. and Bodker, S. (1994) From implementation to design: tailoring and the emergence of systematization, *Computer Supported Cooperative Work*, 10: 45–54.

Trow, M. (1993) Managerialism and the academic profession: the case of England, Institute of Government Studies Working Paper, no. 93-15. Berkeley: University of California.

Wakeford, N. (1999) Gender and the landscapes of computing in an Internet café, in M. Crang, P. Crang and J. May (eds) *Virtual Geographies: Bodies, Space and Relations*. London: Routledge.

Walsh, J.P. and Bayma, T. (1996) Computer networks and scientific work, *Social Studies of Science*, 26: 661–703.

Walsham, G. (2001) *Making a World of Difference: IT in a Global Context*. Chichester: Wiley.

Webster, F. (1995) *Theories of the Information Society*. London: Routledge.

Weick, K.E. (1976) Educational organizations as loosely-coupled systems, *Administrative Science Quarterly*, 21: 1–19.

Wenger, E. (1998) *Communities of Practice*. Cambridge: Cambridge University Press.

Wildavsky, A. (1983) Information as an organizational problem, *Journal of Management Studies*, 20(1): 28–40.

Williams, R. (1997) Universal solutions or local contingencies? Tensions and contradictions in the mutual shaping of technology and work organization, in I. McLoughlin and M. Harris (eds) *Innovation, Organizational Change and Technology*. London: ITB Press, 170–85.

Winner, L. (1998) *Automatic Professor Machine*. Available at http://www.rpi.edu/~winner/apm1.html (accessed 6 June 1999).

Woolgar, S. (ed.) (1988) *Knowledge and Reflexivity. New Frontiers in the Sociology of Knowledge*. London: Sage.

Woolgar, S. and Cooper, G. (1999) Do artefacts have ambivalence? Moses' bridges, Winner's bridges and other urban legends in S&TS, *Social Studies of Science*, 29(3): 433–49.

Index

The Society for Research into Higher Education

The Society for Research into Higher Education (SRHE), an international body, exists to stimulate and coordinate research into all aspects of higher education. It aims to improve the quality of higher education through the encouragement of debate and publication on issues of policy, on the organization and management of higher education institutions, and on the curriculum, teaching and learning methods.

The Society is entirely independent and receives no subsidies, although individual events often receive sponsorship from business or industry. The Society is financed through corporate and individual subscriptions and has members from many parts of the world. It is an NGO of UNESCO.

Under the imprint *SRHE & Open University Press*, the Society is a specialist publisher of research, having over 80 titles in print. In addition to *SRHE News*, the Society's newsletter, the Society publishes three journals: *Studies in Higher Education* (three issues a year), *Higher Education Quarterly* and *Research into Higher Education Abstracts* (three issues a year).

The Society runs frequent conferences, consultations, seminars and other events. The annual conference in December is organized at and with a higher education institution. There are a growing number of networks which focus on particular areas of interest, including:

Access	Learning Environment
Assessment	Legal Education
Consultants	Managing Innovation
Curriculum Development	New Technology for Learning
Eastern European	Postgraduate Issues
Educational Development Research	Quantitative Studies
FE/HE	Student Development
Funding	Vocational Qualifications
Graduate Employment	

Benefits to members

Individual

* The opportunity to participate in the Society's networks
* Reduced rates for the annual conferences

- Free copies of *Research into Higher Education Abstracts*
- Reduced rates for *Studies in Higher Education*
- Reduced rates for *Higher Education Quarterly*
- Free copy of *Register of Members' Research Interests* – includes valuable reference material on research being pursued by the Society's members
- Free copy of occasional in-house publications, e.g. *The Thirtieth Anniversary Seminars Presented by the Vice-Presidents*
- Free copies *SRHE News* which informs members of the Society's activities and provides a calendar of events, with additional material provided in regular mailings
- A 35 per cent discount on all SRHE/Open University Press books
- The opportunity for you to apply for the annual research grants
- Inclusion of your research in the *Register of Members' Research Interests*

Corporate

- Reduced rates for the annual conferences
- The opportunity for members of the Institution to attend SRHE's network events at reduced rates
- Free copies of *Research into Higher Education Abstracts*
- Free copies of *Studies in Higher Education*
- Free copies of *Register of Members' Research Interests* – includes valuable reference material on research being pursued by the Society's members
- Free copy of occasional in-house publications
- Free copies of *SRHE News*
- A 35 per cent discount on all SRHE/Open University Press books
- The opportunity for members of the Institution to submit applications for the Society's research grants
- The opportunity to work with the Society and co-host conferences
- The opportunity to include in the *Register of Members' Research Interests* your Institution's research into aspects of higher education

Membership details: SRHE, 76 Portland Place, London W1B 1NT, UK Tel: 020 7637 2766. Fax: 020 7637 2781.
email: srhe@mailbox.ulcc.ac.uk
world wide web: http://www.srhe.ac.uk/srhe/
Catalogue: SRHE & Open University Press, Celtic Court, 22 Ballmoor, Buckingham MK18 1XW.
Tel: 01280 823388. Fax: 01280 823233. email:
enquiries@openup.co.uk

MAKING SENSE OF ACADEMIC LIFE
ACADEMICS, UNIVERSITIES AND CHANGE

Peter G. Taylor

This book helps academics to become players rather than pawns in the process of change. To do so it raises issues that might inform thinking about – and therefore reactions to – academics' experiences of their changing roles in changing universities.

In universities, the tradition *is* to change. The author looks at the big picture of change in higher education, and in academics' work and work environments. The focus is on the emergent educational role of academics, and the relationship between academics and their institutions.

In these times, the strategy of working harder will not work. Unlike books written about how universities might be better managed, this book explores issues of self-interested self-management for academics. It suggests new ways of thinking about the nature and future of academic work, particularly in terms of the relationship between academic and institutional values, priorities and practices.

Making Sense of Academic Life makes fascinating reading for all those interested in the evolving roles of academics and especially for academics themselves, aspiring academics, and academic managers.

Contents
Setting the scene – Visions of the past and of the future – Academics' work and working – Issues of leadership and management – Academics new work – How may we be? – Moving on – References – Index – The Society for Research into Higher Education.

192pp   0 335 20184 9 (Paperback)   0335 20185 7 (Hardback)

CHALLENGING KNOWLEDGE

Gerard Delanty

For far too long, we have waited for a book that recorded the ideas of the modern university. Now, in Gerard Delanty's new book, we have it. Delanty has faithfully set out the views of the key thinkers and, in the process, has emerged with an idea of the university that is his. We are in his debt.

Professor Ronald Barnett, University of London

Gerard Delanty is one of the most productive and thought-provoking social theorists currently writing in the UK. He brings to his works a sophisticated and impressively cosmopolitan vision. Here he turns his attention to higher education, bringing incisive analysis and a surprising optimism as regards the future of the university. This is a book which will stimulate all thinking people – especially those trying to come to terms with mass higher education and its tribulations.

Professor Frank Webster, University of Birmingham

For too long social theory, the sociology of knowledge and studies in higher education have mutually ignored each other. Gerard Delanty, founding editor of the European Journal of Social Theory, was just the right person to bring them into dialogue. Indeed, 'dialogue' and 'communication' are his watchwords for revamping the institutional mission of the university.

Professor Steve Fuller, University of Warwick

Drawing from current debates in social theory about the changing nature of knowledge, this book offers the most comprehensive sociological theory of the university that has yet appeared. Delanty views the university as a key institution of modernity and as the site where knowledge, culture and society interconnect. He assesses the question of the crisis of the university with respect to issues such as globalization, the information age, the nation state, academic capitalism, cultural politics and changing relationships between research and teaching. Arguing against the notion of the demise of the university, his argument is that in the knowledge society of today a new identity for the university is emerging based on communication and new conceptions of citizenship. It will be essential reading for those interested in changing relationships between modernity, knowledge, higher education and the future of the university.

Contents

192pp   0 335 20578 X (Paperback)   0 335 20579 8 (Hardback)

MODERNISING THE WELFARE STATE

WELFARE STATE

The Blair legacy

Edited by Martin Powell

LIBRARY AND L

This edition published in Great Britain in 2008 by

The Policy Press
University of Bristol
Fourth Floor
Beacon House
Queen's Road
Bristol BS8 1QU
UK

Tel +44 (0)117 331 4054
Fax +44 (0)117 331 4093
e-mail tpp-info@bristol.ac.uk
www.policypress.org.uk

British Library Cataloguing in Publication Data
A catalogue record for this book is available from the British Library.

Library of Congress Cataloging-in-Publication Data
A catalog record for this book has been requested.

ISBN 978 1 84742 039 8 paperback
ISBN 978 1 84742 040 4 hardcover

The right of Martin Powell to be identified as editor of this work has been
asserted by him in accordance with the 1988 Copyright, Designs and Patents
Act.

Cover design by Robin Hawes.
Front cover: image kindly supplied by Getty Images.
Printed and bound in Great Britain by Hobbs the Printers, Southampton.